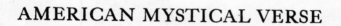

AMERICAN MYSTICAL VERSE

AMERICAN MYSTICAL VERSE ✭ AN ANTHOLOGY SELECTED *By* IRENE HUNTER ✭ PREFACE *By* ZONA GALE ✭

Granger Index Reprint Series

BOOKS FOR LIBRARIES PRESS
FREEPORT, NEW YORK

STANDARD BOOK NUMBER:
8369-6148-X

LIBRARY OF CONGRESS CATALOG CARD NUMBER:
79-116407

MANUFACTURED
BY
HALLMARK LITHOGRAPHERS, INC.
IN THE U.S.A.

PREFACE

Some years ago Anna Hempstead Branch, Pauline F. J. Brower and another considered assembling a volume of American Mystical Verse. The book was to follow the principle of the *Oxford Book of English Mystical Verse*, that is, selection was to be made from among those poets alone whose expression touched toward that heightened perception, that enlargement of vision and level of being, which is so variously denominated. The death of Mrs. Brower prevented the carrying out of this project, which has now been so beautifully achieved by Irene Louise Hunter, who was a young poet and mystic of Riverside, California. Miss Hunter died on her birthday anniversary, July 1, 1924, on the day on which the letter was dated accepting for publication her collection.

The work was done over a period of two years, and chiefly from the bed to which a painful illness confined her. It was in a room looking toward Mount Rubidoux, the right setting for her rapt

PREFACE

beauty. She lived intensely in this work, and the spirit of the theory which led her was something like this:

That just as there are those with a genius for learning or for the arts, so there are those others who have a genius for contacting a subtler reality. And this reality has not to do with ethics nor any system of religion, but rather with a special grace of perception of certain intangible aspects of being. Such people, questioned, have no intellectual replies, because their apprehension in this respect is not an intellectual process. The only possible method to arrive at this area of their contact is to share in that perception. Now, in music, in color, in pure form this special divination is recognized and allowed, and wisdom in music, color or form may be imparted only if the student has the discernment to contact such beauty. But in the domain of the spirit, common opinion which respects the inner faculty of the musician or the artist, permits no specialism.

Nevertheless, these specialists, as Balzac named them, for ages, here and there in the world, have pursued their lives of immediate contact with an inner flame. To some extent, all creative effort partakes of their faculty. Sometimes they have tried to picture it, sometimes they have written of

PREFACE

it. Recently color and music and geometry have expressed some of its borders. And of those who have tried to catch its faint presence in verse are the poets whom Irene Hunter* has chosen to spin the substance of her book.

Preëminently she was one to assemble these poems, because she herself contacted truth in this exquisite way. As the antennæ of the radio draw sound, and as the new science extracts electricity from the air, so she distils from delicate interstices those values which, for eyes like hers, burn and vanish, but leave their aroma. Of such aromas she has made her anthology, as she has made her life.

ZONA GALE

---

* Irene Louise Hunter, 1885-1924. Daughter of William Armstrong Hunter, D.D., Ph.D., and of Eliza Chambers Hunter. Born in Toronto; A.B., Colorado College, 1909. Her successive ambitions, music, missionary career, the teaching of Spanish, literature, were in turn blocked by invalidism. For fifteen years a resident of Riverside, California.

vii

CONTENTS

CONTENTS

CONTENTS

CONTENTS

ACKNOWLEDGMENTS

For permission to use copyrighted material included in this volume, the compiler is indebted to the following authors and publishers, whose courtesy is hereby gratefully acknowledged:

A. S. Barnes and Company, the poem by Ray Palmer.

The Century Company, the poems by Cale Young Rice, James Oppenheim and Helen Keller.

DeWolfe, Fiske and Company, the poem by Sarah P. M. Greene.

Dodd, Mead and Company, the poems by Paul Lawrence Dunbar, Hazel Hall, Angela Morgan, and Richard Le Gallienne.

George H. Doran Company, the poem by Elinor Wylie.

Doubleday, Page and Company, the poems by Walt Whitman.

E. P. Dutton and Company, the poems by Phillips Brooks and Willard Wattles.

Funk and Wagnalls, the poem by Richard Realf.

Harcourt, Brace and Company, Inc., the poems by Margaret Widdemer and George E. Woodberry.

Henry Holt and Company, the poems by George Sterling.

Houghton Mifflin and Company, the poems by Anna Hempstead Branch, John Burroughs, Alice

Cary, Ralph Waldo Emerson, Richard Watson
Gilder, Louise Imogene Guiney, Oliver Wendell
Holmes, William Dean Howells, Lucy Larcom, Henry
Wadsworth Longfellow, Caroline A. Mason, William
Vaughan Moody, Josephine Preston Peabody,
Robert Schauffler, E. R. Sill, Harriet Beecher Stowe,
Edith M. Thomas, Henry D. Thoreau, John Green-
leaf Whittier.

B. W. Huebsch, the poem by William Ellery
Leonard.

Mitchell Kennerley, the poems by Shaemas O'Sheel
and Edna St. Vincent Millay.

Alfred A. Knopf, Inc., the poems by Stephen
Graham.

Little, Brown and Company, the poems by Louise
Chandler Moulton and Emily Dickinson.

The Macmillan Company, the poems by Madison J.
Cawein, Fanny Stearns Davis, Nicholas Vachel Lind-
say, Zona Gale and Alice Brown.

Thomas B. Mosher, the poems by Lizette Wood-
worth Reese.

Joel Munsell's Sons, the poem by George Washing-
ton Doane.

G. P. Putnam's Sons, the poem by David Morton.

Charles Scribner's Sons, the poems by Maltbie
Davenport Babcock, Eugene Field, Sidney Lanier,
Henry van Dyke, John Hall Wheelock, Ridgley Tor-
rence, George Santayana and George E. Woodberry.

Small Maynard and Company, the poems by Rich-
ard Hovey and John Bannister Tabb.

Yale University Press, the poems by William Alex-

ACKNOWLEDGMENTS

ander Percy, Lee Wilson Dodd and William Rose
Benet.

The editors are deeply grateful to the following
poets, editors, magazines, and individual holders
of copyright for permission graciously given to
use the following poems:

America, for permission to use "Quo Vadis" by
Myles Connolly.

Madison Cawein, for permission to use "Pentralia"
by Madison Julius Cawein.

Contemporary Verse, for permission to use "Mani-
festations" by Hilda Morris.

Fannie S. Gifford, for permission to use "Profits"
by Fannie Stearns Davis.

Sarah Greene, for permission to use "De Massa ob
de Sheepfol'" by Sarah Greene.

Good Housekeeping, for permission to use "Retri-
bution" by Violet Alleyn Storey.

Ruth Hall, for permission to use "The Thin Door"
by Hazel Hall.

Mildred Howells, for permission to use "Earliest
Spring" by William Dean Howells.

Thomas S. Jones, Jr., for permission to use "Joyous
Gard," from "The Rose Jar," by Thomas S. Jones, Jr.

Helen Keller, for permission to use "In the Gar-
den of the Lord" by Helen Keller.

Nicholas Vachel Lindsay, for permission to use
"The Heart of God" and "The Soul of the City" by
Nicholas Vachel Lindsay.

AMERICAN MYSTICAL VERSE

The *Lyric*, for permission to use "The Troubadour of God" by Charles Wharton Stork, and "A Fragment" by William Alexander Percy.

Edwin Markham, for permission to use "The Whirlwind Road" and "The Invisible Bride," from *The Man With the Hoe and Other Poems*, by Edwin Markham.

Edna St. Vincent Millay, for permission to use the selection from "Renascence," and "O World I Cannot Hold Thee Close Enough" by Edna St. Vincent Millay.

Kenneth Morris, for permission to use "Dusk" by Kenneth Morris.

David Morton, for permission to use "Symbol" by David Morton.

The New Republic, for permission to use "Concert Pitch" by Conrad Aiken.

North American Review, for permission to use "Somewhere I Know" by Joseph Auslander.

James Oppenheim, for permission to use "Not Overlooked," "Listen," and "I Could Write the Psalms Again" by James Oppenheim.

Shaemas O'Sheel, for permission to use "He Whom a Dream Hath Possessed" and "They Went Forth to Battle" by Shaemas O'Sheel.

The Outlook Company, for permission to use "The White Comrade" by Robert Haven Schauffler.

Cale Young Rice, for permission to use "Providence," from "Wraiths and Realities," by Cale Young Rice.

Alexander M. Robertson, for permission to use "In

ACKNOWLEDGMENTS

Autumn" and "Omnia Exeunt in Mysterium" by George Sterling.

Clinton Scollard, for permission to use "Sanctuary" and "Come, Courage, Come" by Clinton Scollard.

Robert Haven Schauffler, for permission to use "The White Comrade" by Robert Haven Schauffler.

Charles Wharton Stork, for permission to use "The Troubadour of God" and "God, You Have Been Too Good to Me" by Charles Wharton Stork.

George Sterling, for permission to use "In Autumn" and "Omnia Exeunt in Mysterium" by George Sterling.

The Sun, for permission to use "God, You Have Been Too Good to Me" by Charles Wharton Stork.

Ridgeley Torrence, for permission to use "Eye-Witness" and "Headland Orchards" by Ridgley Torrence.

G. O. Warren, for permission to use "Once More" by G. O. Warren.

George E. Woodberry, for permission to use "O Ecstasy" and "Immortal Love" by George E. Woodberry.

Margaret Widdemer, for permission to use "The Other Place" by Margaret Widdemer.

The Yale Review, for permission to use "Sonnet" by Clement Wood.

AMERICAN
MYSTICAL VERSE

TO A WATERFOWL

WHITHER, midst falling dew,
    While glow the heavens with the last
        steps of day,
Far, through their rosy depths, dost thou pursue
    Thy solitary way?

    Vainly the fowler's eye
Might mark thy distant flight to do thee wrong,
As, darkly seen against the crimson sky,
    Thy figure floats along.

    Seek'st thou the plashy brink

NOTE: From the collected poems of William Cullen
Bryant, published by D. Appleton and Company.

Of weedy lake, or marge of river wide,
Or where the rocking billows rise and sink
  On the chafed ocean-side?

  There is a Power whose care
Teaches thy way along that pathless coast—
The desert and illimitable air—
  Lone wandering, but not lost.

  All day thy wings have fanned,
At that far height, the cold, thin atmosphere,
Yet stoop not, weary, to the welcome land,
  Though the dark night is near.

  And soon that toil shall end;
Soon shalt thou find a summer home, and rest,
And scream among thy fellows; reeds shall bend,
  Soon, o'er thy sheltered nest.

  Thou'rt gone, the abyss of heaven

TO A WATERFOWL

Hath swallowed up thy form; yet, on my heart

Deeply hath sunk the lesson thou hast given,

   And shall not soon depart.

   He who, from zone to zone,

Guides through the boundless sky thy certain

      flight,

In the long way that I must tread alone,

   Will lead my steps aright.

WILLIAM CULLEN BRYANT
1794-1878

EVENING

SOFTLY now the light of day
    Fades upon my sight away;
Free from care, from labor free,
Lord, I would commune with Thee.

Thou, whose all-pervading eye
Naught escapes, without, within,
Pardon each infirmity,
Open fault, and secret sin.

Soon, for me, the light of day
Shall forever pass away;
Then, from sin and sorrow free,
Take me, Lord, to dwell with Thee:

4

EVENING

Thou, who sinless, yet has known

All of man's infirmity;

Then, from Thine eternal throne,

Jesus, look with pitying eye.

George Washington Doane
1799-1859

From THRENODY

WILT thou not ope thy heart to know
What rainbows teach, and sunsets
show?
Verdict which accumulates
From lengthening scroll of human fates,
Voice of earth to earth returned,
Prayers of saints that inly burned,—
Saying, *What is excellent,*
As God lives, is permanent;
Hearts are dust, hearts' loves remain;
Heart's love will meet thee again.
Revere the Maker; fetch thine eye
Up to His style, and manners of the sky.
Not of adamant and gold
Built He heaven stark and cold;

THRENODY

No, but a nest of bending reeds,

Flowering grass and scented weeds;

Or like a traveler's fleeing tent,

Or bow above the tempest bent;

Built of tears and sacred flames,

And virtue reaching to its aims;

Built of furtherance and pursuing,

Not of spent deeds, but of doing.

Silent rushes the swift Lord

Through ruined systems still restored,

Broadsowing, bleak and void to bless,

Plants with worlds the wilderness;

Waters with tears of ancient sorrow

Apples of Eden ripe to-morrow.

House and tenant go to ground,

Lost in God, in Godhead found.

Ralph Waldo Emerson
1803-1882

EACH AND ALL

LITTLE thinks, in the field, yon red-cloaked
    clown
Of thee from the hilltop looking down;
The heifer that lows in the upland farm,
Far-heard, lows not thine ear to charm;
The sexton, tolling his bell at noon,
Deems not that great Napoleon
Stops his horse, and lists with delight,
Whilst his files sweep round yon Alpine height;
Nor knowest thou what argument
Thy life to thy neighbor's creed has lent.
All are needed by each one;
Nothing is fair or good alone.
I thought the sparrow's note from heaven,
Singing at dawn on the alder bough;

EACH AND ALL

I brought him home, in his nest, at even;

He sings the song, but it cheers not now,

For I did not bring home the river and sky;—

He sang to my ear,—they sang to my eye.

The delicate shells lay on the shore;

The bubbles of the latest wave

Fresh pearls to their enamel gave,

And the bellowing of the savage sea

Greeted their safe escape to me.

I wiped away the weeds and foam,

I fetched my sea-born treasures home;

But the poor, unsightly, noisome things

Had left their beauty on the shore,

With the sun and the sand and the wild uproar.

The lover watched his graceful maid,

As 'mid the virgin train she strayed;

Nor knew her beauty's best attire
Was woven still by the snow-white choir.
At last she came to his hermitage,
Like the bird from the woodlands to the cage;—
The gay enchantment was undone,
A gentle wife, but fairy none.

Then I said, "I covet truth;
Beauty is unripe childhood's cheat;
I leave it behind with the games of youth:—"
As I spoke, beneath my feet
The ground-pine curled its pretty wreath,
Running over the club-moss burrs;
I inhaled the violet's breath;
Around me stood the oaks and firs;
Pine-cones and acorns lay on the ground;
Over me soared the eternal sky,

EACH AND ALL

Full of light and of deity;

Again I saw, again I heard,

The rolling river, the morning bird;—

Beauty through my senses stole;

I yielded myself to the perfect whole.

RALPH WALDO EMERSON
1803-1882

THE RHODORA

ON BEING ASKED WHENCE IS THE FLOWER

IN May, when sea winds pierced our solitudes,
   I found the fresh Rhodora in the woods,
Spreading its leafless blooms in a damp nook,
To please the desert and the sluggish brook.
The purple petals, fallen in the pool,
Made the black water with their beauty gay;
Here might the redbird come his plumes to cool,
And court the flower that cheapens his array.
Rhodora! if the sages ask thee why
This charm is wasted on the earth and sky,
Tell them, dear, that if eyes were made for seeing,
Then Beauty is its own excuse for being:
Why thou wert there, O rival of the rose!

THE RHODORA

I never thought to ask, I never knew:

But, in my simple ignorance, suppose

The selfsame Power that brought me there

    brought you.

RALPH WALDO EMERSON
1803-1882

From FRAGMENTS

LET me go where'er I will
    I hear a sky-born music still;
It sounds from all things old,
It sounds from all things young,
From all that's fair, from all that's foul,
Peals out a cheerful song.

It is not only in the rose,
It is not only in the bird,
Not only where the rainbow glows,
Nor in the song of woman heard,
But in the darkest, meanest things
There alway, alway, something sings.

'Tis not in the high stars alone,
Nor in the cups of budding flowers,

FRAGMENTS

Nor in the redbreast's mellow tone,

Nor in the bow that smiles in showers,

But in the mud and scum of things

There alway, alway something sings.

RALPH WALDO EMERSON
1803-1882

WORSHIP

THIS is he, who, felled by foes,
    Sprung harmless up, refreshed by
    blows!
He to captivity was sold,
But him no prison-bars would hold:
Though they sealed him in a rock,
Mountain chains he can unlock:
Thrown to lions for their meat,
The crouching lion kissed his feet:
Bound to the stake, no flames appalled,
But arched o'er him an honoring vault.
This is he men miscall! Fate,
Threading dark ways, arriving late,

WORSHIP

But ever coming in time to crown
The truth, and hurl wrongdoers down.
He is the oldest, and best known,
More near than aught thou call'st thy own,
Yet, greeted in another's eyes,
Disconcerts with glad surprise.
This is Jove, who, deaf to prayers,
Floods with blessings unawares.
Draw, if thou canst, the mystic line
Severing rightly his from thine,
Which is human, which divine.

RALPH WALDO EMERSON
1803-1882

THE UNDERSONG

From WOODNOTES

'HEED the old oracles,
    Ponder my spells;
Song wakes in my pinnacles
When the wind swells.
Soundeth the prophetic wind,
The shadows shake on the rock behind,
And the countless leaves of the pine are strings
Tuned to the lay the wood-god sings.
    Hearken! Hearken!
If thou wouldst know the mystic song
Chanted when the sphere was young.
Aloft, abroad, the pæan swells;
O wise man! hear'st thou half it tells?

THE UNDERSONG

O wise man! hear'st thou the least part?

'Tis the chronicle of art.

To the open ear it sings

Sweet the genesis of things,

Of tendency through endless ages,

Of star-dust, and star-pilgrimages,

Of rounded worlds, of space and time,

Of the old flood's subsiding slime,

Of chemic matter, force and form,

Of poles and powers, cold, wet and warm:

The rushing metamorphosis

Dissolving all that fixture is,

Melts things that be to things that seem,

And solid nature to a dream.

O, listen to the undersong,

The ever old, the ever young;

And, far within those cadent pauses,

AMERICAN MYSTICAL VERSE

The chorus of the ancient Causes!

Delights the dreadful Destiny

To fling his voice into the tree,

And shock thy weak ear with a note

Breathed from the everlasting throat.

In music he repeats the pang

Whence the fair flock of Nature sprang.

O mortal! thy ears are stones;

These echoes are laden with tones

Which only the pure can hear;

Thou canst not catch what they recite

Of Fate and Will, of Want and Right,

Of man to come, of human life,

Of Death and Fortune, Growth and Strife.'

RALPH WALDO EMERSON
1803-1882

THE MIGHTY HEART
From Woodnotes

COME learn with me the fatal song
     Which knits the world in music
          strong,
Come lift thine eyes to lofty rhymes,
Of things with things, of times with times,
Primal chimes of sun and shade,
Of sound and echo, man and maid,
The land reflected in the flood,
Body with shadow still pursued.

For Nature beats in perfect tune,
And rounds with rhyme her every rune,
Whether she work in land or sea,
Or hide underground her alchemy.
Thou canst not wave thy staff in air,

Or dip thy paddle in the lake,

But it carves the bow of beauty there,

And the ripples in rhymes the oar forsake.

The wood is wiser far than thou;

The wood and wave each other know,

Not unrelated, unified,

But to each thought and thing allied,

Is perfect Nature's every part,

Rooted in the mighty Heart.

But thou, poor child! unbound, unrhymed,

Whence camest thou, misplaced, mistimed,

Whence, O thou orphan and defrauded?

Is thy land peeled, thy realm marauded?

Who thee divorced, deceived and left?

Thee of thy faith who hath bereft,

And torn the ensigns from thy brow,

And sunk the immortal eye so low?

THE MIGHTY HEART

Thy cheek too white, thy form too slender,

Thy gait too slow, thy habits tender

For royal man—they thee confess

An exile from the wilderness,—

The hills where health with health agrees,

And the wise soul expels disease.

Hark! in thy ear I will tell the sign

By which thy hurt thou may'st divine.

When thou shalt climb the mountain cliff,

Or see the wide shore from thy skiff,

To thee the horizon shall express

But emptiness on emptiness;

There lives no man of Nature's worth

In the circle of the earth;

And to thine eye the vast skies fall,

Dire and satirical,

On clucking hens and prating fools,

On thieves, on drudges, and on dolls.

And thou shalt say to the Most High,

"Godhead! all this astronomy,

And fate and practice and invention,

Strong art and beautiful pretension,

This radiant pomp of sun and star,

Throes that were, and worlds that are,

Behold! were in vain and in vain;—

It cannot be,—I will look again.

Surely now will the curtain rise,

And earth's fit tenant me surprise;—

But the curtain doth *not* rise,

And Nature has miscarried wholly

Into failure, into folly."

'Alas! thine is the bankruptcy,

Blessed Nature so to see.

Come, lay thee in my soothing shade,

24

THE MIGHTY HEART

And heal the hurts which sin has made.

I see thee in the crowd alone;

I will be thy companion.

Quit thy friends as the dead in doom,

And build to them a final tomb;

Let the starred shade that nightly falls

Still celebrate their funerals,

And the bell of beetle and of bee

Knell their melodious memory.

Behind thee leave thy merchandise,

Thy churches and thy charities;

And leave thy peacock wit behind;

Enough for thee the primal mind

That flows in streams, that breathes in wind;

Leave all thy pedant lore apart;

God hid the whole world in thy heart.'

RALPH WALDO EMERSON
1803-1882

25

THE PROBLEM

*　　*　　*　　*　　*　　*　　*　　*

NOT from a vain or shallow thought
　　His awful Jove young Phidias brought;
Never from lips of cunning fell
The thrilling Delphic oracle;
Out from the heart of nature rolled
The burdens of the Bible old;
The litanies of nations came,
Like the volcano's tongue of flame,
Up from the burning core below,—
The canticles of love and woe;
The hand that rounded Peter's dome,
And groined the aisles of Christian Rome,
Wrought in a sad sincerity;

THE PROBLEM

Himself from God he could not free;
He builded better than he knew;—
The conscious stone to beauty grew.

*   *   *   *   *   *   *   *

These temples grew as grows the grass;
Art might obey, but not surpass.
The passive Master lent his hand
To the vast soul that o'er him planned;
And the same power that reared the shrine,—
Bestrode the tribes that knelt within.
Ever the fiery Pentecost
Girds with one flame the countless host,
Trances the heart through chanting choirs,
And through the priest the mind inspires.

The word unto the prophet spoken
Was writ on tables yet unbroken;
The word by seers and sibyls told,

AMERICAN MYSTICAL VERSE

In groves of oak, or fanes of gold,

Still floats upon the morning wind,

Still whispers to the willing mind.

One accent of the Holy Ghost

The heedless world hath never lost.

*   *   *   *   *   *   *   *

RALPH WALDO EMERSON
1803-1882

DIVINA COMMEDIA

OFT have I seen at some cathedral door
A laborer, passing in the dust and heat,
Lay down his burden, and with reverent feet,
Enter, and cross himself, and on the floor
Kneel to repeat his paternoster o'er;
Far off the noises of the world retreat;
The loud vociferations of the street
Become an indistinguishable roar.
So, as I enter here from day to day,
And leave my burden at this minster gate,
Kneeling in prayer and not ashamed to pray,
The tumult of the time disconsolate
To inarticulate murmurs dies away,
While the eternal ages watch and wait.

HENRY WADSWORTH LONGFELLOW
1807-1882

NATURE

A S a fond mother, when the day is o'er,
Leads by the hand her little child to bed,
Half willing, half reluctant to be led,
And leave his broken playthings on the floor,
Still gazing at them through the open door,
Nor wholly reassured and comforted
By promises of others in their stead,
Which, though more splendid, may not please him
more ;
So Nature deals with us, and takes away
Our playthings one by one, and by the hand
Leads us to rest so gently, that we go
Scarce knowing if we wish to go or stay,

NATURE

Being too full of sleep to understand

How far the unknown transcends the what we

know.

HENRY WADSWORTH LONGFELLOW
1807-1882

From THE ETERNAL GOODNESS

I KNOW not what the future hath
   Of marvel or surprise,
Assured alone that life and death
   His mercy underlies.

And if my heart and flesh are weak
   To bear an untried pain,
The bruisèd reed He will not break,
   But strengthen and sustain.
* * * * * * * *
And so beside the Silent Sea
   I wait the muffled oar;
No harm from Him can come to me
   On ocean or on shore.

THE ETERNAL GOODNESS

I know not where His islands lift
　　Their fronded palms in air;
I only know I cannot drift
　　Beyond His love and care.

O brothers! if my faith is vain,
　　If hopes like these betray,
Pray for me that my feet may gain
　　The sure and safer way.

And Thou, O Lord! by whom are seen
　　Thy creatures as they be,
Forgive me if too close I lean
　　My human heart on Thee!

JOHN GREENLEAF WHITTIER
1807-1892

33

From OUR MASTER

IMMORTAL Love, forever full,
　　Forever flowing free,
Forever shared, forever whole,
　　A never-ebbing sea!

*　　*　　*　　*　　*　　*　　*　　*

We may not climb the heavenly steeps
　　To bring the Lord Christ down;
In vain we search the lowest deeps,
　　For Him no depths can drown.

*　　*　　*　　*　　*　　*　　*　　*

The letter fails, and systems fall,
　　And every symbol wanes;
The Spirit over-brooding all
　　Eternal Love remains.

34

OUR MASTER

And not for signs in heaven above
 Or earth below they look,
Who knows with John His smile of love,
 With Peter His rebuke.

In joy of inward peace, or sense
 Of sorrow over sin,
He is His own best evidence,
 His witness is within.

No fable old, nor mythic lore,
 Nor dream of bards and seers,
No dead fact stranded on the shore
 Of the oblivious years;—

But warm, sweet, tender, even yet
 A present help is He;
And faith has still its Olivet
 And love its Galilee.

35

AMERICAN MYSTICAL VERSE

The healing of His seamless dress
  Is by our beds of pain;
We touch Him in life's throng and press,
  And we are whole again.

Through Him the first fond prayers are said
  Our lips of childhood frame,
The last low whispers of our dead
  Are burdened with His name.

O Lord and Master of us all!
  Whate'er our name or sign,
We own Thy sway, we hear Thy call,
  We test our lives by Thine.

JOHN GREENLEAF WHITTIER
1807-1892

INSPIRATION

IF with light head erect I sing,
   Though all the Muses lend their force,
From my poor love of anything,
   The verse is weak and shallow as its source.

But if with bended neck I grope,
   Listening behind me for my wit,
With faith superior to hope,
   More anxious to keep back than forward it,—

Making my soul accomplice there
   Unto the flame my heart hath lit,
Then will the verse for ever wear,—
   Time cannot bend the line which God has writ.

I hearing get, who had but ears,

    And sight, who had but eyes before;

I moments live, who lived but years,

    And truth discern, who knew but learning's

        lore.

Now chiefly is my natal hour,

    And only now my prime of life;

Of manhood's strength it is the flower,

    'Tis peace's end, and war's beginning strife.

It comes in summer's broadest noon,

    By a gray wall, or some chance place,

Unseasoning time, insulting June,

    And vexing day with its presuming face.

I will not doubt the love untold

    Which not my worth nor want hath bought,

INSPIRATION

Which woo'd me young, and woos me old,

And to this evening hath me brought.

HENRY DAVID THOREAU
1817-1862

From PASSAGE TO INDIA

PASSAGE, immediate passage! The blood
burns in my veins!

Away, O soul! Hoist instantly the anchor!

Cut the hawsers—haul out—shake out every sail!

Have we not stood here like trees in the ground
long enough?

Have we not grovell'd here long enough, eating
and drinking like mere brutes?

Have we not darkened and daz'd ourselves with
books long enough?

Sail forth—steer for the deep waters only,

Reckless, O soul, exploring, I with thee and thou
with me,

PASSAGE TO INDIA

For we are bound where mariner has not yet
    dared to go,
And we will risk the ship, ourselves and all.

O my brave soul!

O farther farther sail!

O daring joy, but safe! Are they not all the seas
    of God?

O farther, farther, farther sail.

WALT WHITMAN
1819-1892

From PRAYER OF COLUMBUS

MY terminus near,
  The clouds already closing in upon me,
The voyage balk'd, the course disputed, lost,
I yield my ships to Thee.

My hands, my limbs grow nerveless,
My brain feels rack'd, bewildered,
Let the old timbers part, I will not part,
I will cling fast to Thee, O God, though the
  waves buffet me,
Thee, Thee, at least I know.

WALT WHITMAN
1819-1892

42

From THE MYSTIC TRUMPETER

NOW trumpeter! for thy close,
Vouchsafe a higher strain than any yet,
Sing to my soul, renew its languishing faith and
hope,
Rouse up my slow belief, give me some vision
of the future,
Give me for once its prophecy and joy.

O glad, exulting, culminating song!
A vigor more than earth's is in thy notes!
Marches of victory—man disenthralled—the con-
queror at last,
Hymns to the universal God from universal man—
all joy!

AMERICAN MYSTICAL VERSE

A reborn race appears—a perfect world, all joy!

Women and men in wisdom, innocence and health
  —all joy!

Riotous, laughing bacchanals, fill'd with joy!

War, sorrow, suffering, gone—the rank earth
  purged—nothing but joy left!

The ocean filled with joy—the atmosphere all
  joy!

Joy! joy! in freedom, worship, love! joy in the
  ecstasy of life!

Enough to merely be! enough to breathe!

Joy! joy! all over joy!

WALT WHITMAN
1819-1892

44

From SONG OF MYSELF

WHY should I wish to see God better than
this day?

I see something of God each hour of the twenty-
four, and each moment then;

In the faces of men and women I see God, and
in my own face in the glass;

I find letters from God dropt in the street—and
every one is signed by God's name,

And I leave them where they are, for I know that
whereso'er I go,

Others will punctually come for ever and ever.

WALT WHITMAN
1819-1892

45

From SALUT AU MONDE

THIS is not my true country; I have lived
banished from my true country—I
now go back there,
I return to the celestial sphere, where every one
goes in his turn.

WALT WHITMAN
1819-1892

THE LAST INVOCATION

AT the last, tenderly,
    From the walls of the powerful fortress'd
      house,
From the clasp of the knitted locks—from the
    keep of the well-closed doors,
Let me be wafted.

Let me glide noiselessly forth;
With the key of softness unlock the locks—with
    a whisper
Set ope the doors, O soul!

Tenderly—be not impatient,
(Strong is your hold, O mortal flesh!
Strong is your hold O love.)

WALT WHITMAN
1819-1892

DAREST THOU NOW, O SOUL

DAREST thou now, O soul,
  Walk out with me toward the unknown
    region,
Where neither ground is for the feet nor any
  path to follow?

No map there, nor guide,
Nor voice sounding, nor touch of human hand,
Nor face with blooming flesh, nor lips, nor eyes,
  are in that land.

I know it not, O soul!
Nor dost thou; all is a blank before us—
All waits undreamed of in that region, that in-
  accessible land.

DAREST THOU NOW, O SOUL

Till when the ties loosen,

All but the ties eternal, Time and Space,

Nor darkness, gravitation, sense, nor any bounds
    bounding us.

Then we burst forth, we float,

In Time and Space, O soul, prepared for them,

Equal, equipped at last, (O joy! O fruit of
    all!) them to fulfill, O soul.

WALT WHITMAN
1819-1892

FAITH

MY faith looks up to Thee,
Thou Lamb of Calvary,
Saviour divine:
Now hear me while I pray,
Take all my guilt away,
O let me from this day
Be wholly Thine.

May Thy rich grace impart
Strength to my fainting heart,
My zeal inspire:
As thou hast died for me,
O may my love to Thee
Pure, warm, and changeless be,—
A living fire.

FAITH

While life's dark maze I tread,

And griefs around me spread,

  Be Thou my guide;

Bid darkness turn to day,

Wipe sorrow's tears away,

Nor let me ever stray

  From Thee aside.

When ends life's transient dream,

When death's cold, sullen stream

  Shall o'er me roll;

Blest Saviour, then, in love,

Fear and distrust remove;

O bear me safe above,—

  A ransomed soul.

RAY PALMER
1808-1887

THE GODDESS'S SONG

From AL AARAAF

SPIRIT! that dwellest where,
   In the deep sky,
The terrible and fair,
   In beauty vie!
Beyond the line of blue—
   The boundary of the star
Which turneth at the view
   Of thy barrier and thy bar—
Of the barrier overgone
   By the comets who were cast
From their pride and from their throne
   To be drudges till the last—

THE GODDESS'S SONG

To be carriers of fire

  (The red fire of their heart)

With speed that may not tire

  And with pain that shall not part—

Who livest—*that* we know—

  In Eternity—we feel—

But the shadow of whose brow

  What spirit shall reveal?

Though the beings whom thy Nesace,

  Thy messenger hath known,

Have dreamed for thy Infinity

  A model of their own—

Thy will is done, O God!

  The star hath ridden high

Through many a tempest, but she rode

  Beneath thy burning eye;

And here, in thought, to thee—

AMERICAN MYSTICAL VERSE

In thought that can alone

Ascend thy empire, and so be

A partner of thy throne—

By wingèd Fantasy,

My embassy is given,

Till secrecy shall knowledge be

In the environs of Heaven.

EDGAR ALLAN POE
1809-1849

HYMN OF TRUST

O LOVE Divine, that stooped to share
　　Our sharpest pang, our bitterest tear,
On Thee we cast each earth-born care,
　　We smile at pain while Thou art near!

Though long the weary way we tread,
　　And sorrow crown each lingering year,
No path we shun, no darkness dread,
　　Our hearts still whispering, "Thou art near!"

When drooping pleasure turns to grief,
　　And trembling faith is changed to fear,
The murmuring wind, the quivering leaf,
　　Shall softly tell us, "Thou art near!"

55

AMERICAN MYSTICAL VERSE

On Thee we fling our burdening woe,

O Love Divine, forever dear,

Content to suffer while we know,

Living and dying, Thou art near!

OLIVER WENDELL HOLMES
1809-1894

WHEN I AWAKE I AM STILL WITH THEE

STILL, still with Thee, when purple morning
    breaketh,
  When the bird waketh and the shadows flee;
Fairer than morning, lovelier than the daylight,
  Dawns the sweet consciousness, I am with
    Thee!

Alone with Thee, amid the mystic shadows,
  The solemn hush of nature newly born;
Alone with Thee, in breathless adoration,
  In the calm dew and freshness of the morn.

Still, still with Thee, as to each new-born morning
  A fresh and solemn splendor still is given,

So doth this blessed consciousness, awakening,

    Breathe, each day, nearness unto Thee and

       heaven.

When sinks the soul, subdued by toil, to slumber,

    Its closing eye looks up to Thee in prayer;

Sweet the respose beneath Thy wings o'ershad-

       ing,

    But sweeter still to wake and find Thee there.

So shall it be at last, in that bright morning

    When the soul waketh and life's shadows flee;

O, in that hour fairer than daylight dawning,

    Shall rise the glorious thought, I am with Thee!

HARRIET BEECHER STOWE
1812-1896

"THALATTA! THALATTA!"

CRY OF THE TEN THOUSAND

I STAND upon the summit of my years;
    Behind, the toil, the camp, the march, the
       strife,
The wandering and the desert; vast, afar,
Beyond this weary way, behold! the Sea!
The sea o'er-swept by clouds and winds and
    wings,
By thoughts and wishes manifold, whose breath
Is freshness and whose mighty pulse is peace.
Palter no question of the dim Beyond;
Cut loose the bark; such voyage itself is rest;
Majestic motion, unimpeded scope,

59

A widening heaven, a current without care.

Eternity!—Deliverance, Promise, Course!

Time-tired souls salute thee from the shore.

JOSEPH BROWNLEE BROWN
1824-1888

DYING HYMN

EARTH, with its dark and dreadful ills,
  Recedes, and fades away;
Lift up your heads, ye heavenly hills;
  Ye gates of death, give way!

My soul is full of whispered song,
  My blindness is my sight;
The shadows that I feared so long
  Are all alive with light.

The while my pulses faintly beat,
  My faith doth so abound,
I feel grow firm beneath my feet
  The green immortal ground.

That faith to me a courage gives

   Low as the grave to go:

I know that my Redeemer lives:

   That I shall live, I know.

The palace walls I almost see,

   Where dwells my Lord and King;

O grave, where is thy victory!

   O death, where is thy sting!

ALICE CARY
1820-1871

EVENTIDE

A^T cool of day, with God I walk
    My garden's grateful shade;
I hear His voice among the trees,
    And I am not afraid.

He speaks to me in every wind,
    He smiles from every star;
He is not deaf to me, nor blind,
    Nor absent, nor afar.

His hand, that shuts the flowers to sleep,
    Each in its dewy fold,
Is strong my feeble life to keep,
    And competent to hold.

The powers below and powers above,

    Are subject to His care—

I cannot wander from His love

    Who loves me everywhere.

Thus dowered, and guarded thus, with Him

    I walk this peaceful shade;

I hear His voice among the trees,

    And I am not afraid!

CAROLINE ATHERTON MASON
1823-1890

IMMORTAL

INTO the heaven of Thy heart, O God,
   I lift up my life, like a flower;
Thy light is deep, and Thy love is broad,
   And I am not the child of an hour.

The throb of Thy infinite life I feel
   In every beat of my heart;
Upon me hast Thou set eternity's seal;
   Forever alive as Thou art.

I know not Thy mystery, O my God,
   Nor yet what my own life means,
That feels after Thee, through the mold and
      the sod
   And the darkness that intervenes.

But I know that I live, since I hate the wrong,

The glory of truth can see;

Can cling to the right with a purpose strong,

Can love and can will with Thee.

LUCY LARCOM
1826-1893

OUR CHRIST

IN Christ I feel the heart of God
   Throbbing from heaven through earth;
Life stirs again within the clod,
   Renewed in beauteous birth;
The soul springs up, a flower of prayer,
Breathing His breath out on the air.

In Christ I touch the hand of God,
   From His pure height reached down,
By blessed ways before untrod,
   To lift us to our crown;
Victory that only perfect is
Through loving sacrifice, like His.

Holding His hand, my steadied feet

  May walk the air, the seas;

On life and death His smile falls sweet,

  Lights up all mysteries;

Stranger nor exile can I be

In new worlds where He leadeth me.

LUCY LARCOM
1826-1893

CHARTLESS

I NEVER saw a moor,
    I never saw the sea,
Yet know I how the heather looks,
    And what a wave must be.

I never spoke with God,
    Nor visited in heaven;
Yet certain am I of the spot
    As if the chart were given.

EMILY DICKINSON
1830-1886

SETTING SAIL

EXULTATION is the going
   Of an inland soul to sea—
Past the houses, past the headlands,
   Into deep eternity!

Bred as we, among the mountains,
   Can the sailor understand
The divine intoxication
   Of the first league out from land?

EMILY DICKINSON
1830-1886

THE WORD *

O EARTH! Thou hast not any wind that
blows

Which is not music; every weed of thine

Pressed rightly flows in aromatic wine;

And humble hedge-row flower that grows,

And every little brown bird that doth sing,

Hath something greater than itself, and bears

A living word to every living thing,

Albeit holds the message unawares.

All shapes and sounds have something which is
not

Of them: a spirit broods amid the grass;

* By permission from *Poems* by Richard Realf, copy-
right, 1898, by Funk & Wagnalls Company, New York.

AMERICAN MYSTICAL VERSE

Vague outlines of the Everlasting Thought

Lie in the melting shadows as they pass;

The touch of an eternal presence thrills

The fringes of the sunsets and the hills.

RICHARD REALF
1834-1878

SOME DAY OR OTHER

SOME day or other I shall surely come
   Where true hearts wait for me;
Then let me learn the language of that home
   While here on earth I be,
Lest my poor lips for want of words be dumb
   In that High Company.

                              LOUISE CHANDLER MOULTON
                                    1835-1908

73

THE CHILD OF BETHLEHEM *

O LITTLE town of Bethlehem,
　　How still we see thee lie!
Above thy deep and dreamless sleep
　　The silent stars go by;
　Yet in thy dark streets shineth
　　The everlasting light;
The hopes and fears of all the years
　　Are met in thee to-night.

　For Christ is born of Mary,
　　And, gathered all above,
While mortals sleep, the angels keep
　　Their watch of wondering love.

* By permission from *Christmas Songs and Easter Carols* by Phillips Brooks, copyright by E. P. Dutton and Company.

THE CHILD OF BETHLEHEM

O morning stars! together
　　Proclaim the holy birth!
And praises sing to God the King,
　　And peace to men on earth.

How silently, how silently,
　　The wondrous gift is given!
So God imparts to human hearts
　　The blessings of His heaven.
No ear may hear His coming,
　　But in this world of sin,
Where meek souls will receive Him still,
　　The dear Christ enters in.

O holy Child of Bethlehem!
　　Descend to us, we pray;
Cast out our sin, and enter in,
　　Be born in us to-day.

AMERICAN MYSTICAL VERSE

We hear the Christmas angels

The great glad tidings tell;

Oh, come to us, abide with us,

Our Lord Emmanuel!

PHILLIPS BROOKS
1835-1893

WAITING

SERENE, I fold my hands and wait,
  Nor care for wind, or tide, or sea;
I rave no more 'gainst Time or Fate,
  For, lo! my own shall come to me.

I stay my haste, I make delays,
  For what avails this eager pace?
I stand amid the eternal ways,
  And what is mine shall know my face.

Asleep, awake, by night or day,
  The friends I seek are seeking me;
No wind can drive my bark astray,
  Nor change the tide of destiny.

AMERICAN MYSTICAL VERSE

What matter if I stand alone?

  I wait with joy the coming years;

My heart shall reap where it has sown,

  And garner up its fruit of tears.

The waters know their own and draw

  The brook that springs in yonder height;

So flows the good with equal law

  Unto the soul of pure delight.

The stars come nightly to the sky;

  The tidal wave unto the sea;

Nor time, nor space, nor deep, nor high,

  Can keep my own away from me.

JOHN BURROUGHS
1837-1921

EARLIEST SPRING

TOSSING his mane of snows in wildest
eddies and tangles,
Lion-like, March cometh in, hoarse, with tem-
pestuous breath,
Through all the moaning chimneys, and 'thwart
all the hollows and angles
Round the shuddering house, threating of winter
and death.

But in my heart I feel the life of the wood and
the meadow
Thrilling the pulses that own kindred with fibers
that lift

Bud and blade to the sunward, within the inscrutable shadow,

Deep in the oak's chill core, under the gathering drift.

Nay, to earth's life in mine some prescience, or dream, or desire

(How shall I name it aright?) comes for a moment and goes—

Rapture of life ineffable, perfect—as if in the brier,

Leafless there by my door, trembled a sense of the rose.

WILLIAM DEAN HOWELLS
1837-1919

HOME

THERE lies a little city in the hills;
 White are its roofs, dim is each dwell-
  ing's door,
And peace with perfect rest its bosom fills.

There the pure mist, the pity of the sea,
Comes as a white, soft hand, and reaches o'er
And touches its still face most tenderly.

Unstirred and calm, amid our shifting years,
Lo! where it lies, far from the clash and roar,
With quiet distance blurred, as if through tears.

O heart, that prayest so for God to send
Some loving messenger to go before
And lead the way to where thy longings end,

AMERICAN MYSTICAL VERSE

Be sure, be very sure, that soon will come

His kindest angel, and through that still door

Into the Infinite love will lead thee home.

EDWARD ROWLAND SILL
1841-1887

A BALLAD OF TREES AND THE MASTER

INTO the woods my Master went,
  Clean forspent, forspent.
Into the woods my Master came,
Forspent with love and shame.
But the olives they were not blind to Him;
The little gray leaves were kind to Him;
The thorn-tree had a mind to Him;
When into the woods He came.

Out of the woods my Master went,
And he was well content.
Out of the woods my Master came,
Content with death and shame.

83

When Death and Shame would woo Him last,

From under the trees they drew Him last:

'Twas on a tree they slew Him—last

When out of the woods He came.

SIDNEY LANIER
1842-1881

THE MARSHES OF GLYNN

GLOOMS of the live-oaks, beautiful-
braided and woven
With intricate shades of the vines that myriad-
cloven
Clamber the forks of the multiform boughs,—
Emerald twilights,—
Virginal shy lights,
Wrought of the leaves to allure to the whisper of
vows,
When lovers pace timidly down through the green
colonnades
Of the dim sweet woods, of the dear dark woods,
Of the heavenly woods and glades,

That run to the radiant marginal sand-beach
within
The wide sea-marshes of Glynn;—

Beautiful glooms, soft dusks in the noonday fire,—
Wildwood privacies, closets of lone desire,
Chamber from chamber parted with wavering
arras of leaves,—
Cells for the passionate pleasure of prayer to the
soul that grieves,
Pure with a sense of the passing of saints through
the wood,
Cool for the dutiful weighing of ill with good;—

O braided dusks of the oak and woven shades of
the vine,
While the riotous noonday sun of the June-day
long did shine

THE MARSHES OF GLYNN

Ye held me fast in your heart and I held you fast
    in mine;

But now when the noon is no more, and riot is
    rest,

And the sun is a-wait at the ponderous gate of the
    West,

And the slant yellow beam down the wood-aisle
    doth seem

Like a lane into heaven that leads from a dream,—

Ay, now, when my soul all day hath drunken the
    soul of the oak,

And my heart is at ease from men, and the weari-
    some sound of the stroke

Of the scythe of time and the trowel of trade is
    low,

And belief overmasters doubt, and I know that I
    know,

And my spirit is grown to a lordly great compass
within,

That the length and the breadth and the sweep of
the marshes of Glynn

Will work me no fear like the fear they have
wrought me of yore

When length was fatigue, and when breadth was
but bitterness sore,

And when terror and shrinking and dreary un-
nameable pain

Drew over me out of the merciless miles of the
plain,—

Oh, now, unafraid, I am fain to face
The vast sweet visage of space.
To the edge of the wood I am drawn, I am drawn,
Where the gray beach glimmering runs, as a belt
of the dawn,

88

THE MARSHES OF GLYNN

    For a mete and a mark

    To the forest-dark:—

      So:

Affable live-oak, leaning low,—

Thus—with your favor—soft, with a reverent
    hand,

(Not lightly touching your person, Lord of the
    land!)

Bending your beauty aside, with a step I stand

On the firm-packed sand,

      Free

By a world of marsh that borders a world of sea.

Sinuous southward and sinuous northward the
    shimmering band

Of the sand-beach fastens the fringe of the marsh
    to the folds of the land.

Inward and outward to northward and southward
    the beach-lines linger and curl

As a silver-wrought garment that clings to and
    follows the firm sweet limbs of a girl.

Vanishing, swerving, evermore curving again into
    sight,

Softly the sand-beach wavers away to a dim gray
    looping of light.

And what if behind me to westward the wall of
    the woods stands high?

The world lies east: how ample, the marsh and
    the sea and the sky!

A league and a league of marsh-grass, waist-high,
    broad in the blade,

Green, and all of a height, and unflecked with a
    light or a shade,

Stretch leisurely off, in a pleasant plain,

THE MARSHES OF GLYNN

To the terminal blue of the main.

Oh, what is abroad in the marsh and the terminal
sea?

Somehow my soul seems suddenly free

From the weighing of fate and the sad discussion
of sin,

By the length and the breadth and the sweep of
the marshes of Glynn.

Ye marshes, how candid and simple and nothing-
withholding and free

Ye publish yourselves to the sky and offer your-
selves to the sea!

Tolerant plains, that suffer the sea and the rains
and the sun,

Ye spread and span like the catholic man who
hath mightily won

God out of knowledge and good out of infinite
  pain

And sight out of blindness and purity out of a
  stain.

As the marsh-hen secretly builds on the watery
  sod,

Behold I will build me a nest on the greatness of
  God:

I will fly in the greatness of God as the marsh-hen
  flies

In the freedom that fills all the space 'twixt the
  marsh and the skies:

By so many roots as the marsh-grass sends in the
  sod

I will heartily lay me a-hold on the greatness of
  God:

THE MARSHES OF GLYNN

Oh, like to the greatness of God is the greatness
    within
The range of the marshes, the liberal marshes of
    Glynn.

And the sea lends large, as the marsh: lo, out of
    his plenty the sea
Pours fast: full soon the time of the flood tide
    must be:
Look how the grace of the sea doth go
About and about through the intricate channels
    that flow
        Here and there,
        Everywhere,
Till his waters have flooded the uttermost creeks
    and the low-lying lanes,
And the marsh is meshed with a million veins,

That like as with rosy and silvery essences flow

In the rose-and-silver evening glow.

Farewell, my lord Sun!

The creeks overflow: a thousand rivulets run

'Twixt the roots of the sod; the blades of the
    marsh-grass stir;

Passeth a hurrying sound of wings that westward
    whirr;

Passeth, and all is still; and the currents cease to
    run;

And the sea and the marsh are one.

How still the plains of the waters be!

The tide is in his ecstasy;

The tide is at his highest height:

And it is night.

THE MARSHES OF GLYNN

And now from the Vast of the Lord will the
  waters of sleep

Roll in the souls of men,

But who will reveal to our waking ken

The forms that swim and the shapes that creep
  under the waters of sleep?

And I would I could know what swimmeth below
  when the tide comes in

On the length and the breadth of the marvelous
  marshes of Glynn.

SIDNEY LANIER
1842-1881

HOLY LAND

THIS is the earth He walked on; not alone
That Asian country keeps the sacred
stain;

Ah, not alone the far Judæan plain,

Mountain and river! Lo, the sun that shone

On Him, shines now on us; when day is gone

The moon of Galilee comes forth again,

And lights our path as His; an endless chain

Of years and sorrows makes the round world
one.

The air we breathe, He breathed—the very air

That took the mold and music of His high

And Godlike speech. Since then shall mortal
dare

HOLY LAND

With base thought front the ever sacred sky—
Soil with foul deed the ground whereon He laid,
In holy death, His pale immortal head!

RICHARD WATSON GILDER
1844-1909

"EACH MOMENT HOLY IS"

EACH moment holy is, for out from God
 Each moment flashes forth a human soul.
Holy each moment is, for back to Him
Some wandering soul each moment home returns.

RICHARD WATSON GILDER
1844-1909

LONE-LAND

AROUND us lies a world invisible,
   With isles of dreams and many a con-
      tinent
Of Thought, and Isthmus Fancy, where we dwell
   Each as a lonely wanderer intent
Upon his vision; finding each his fears
And hopes encompassed by the tide of Tears.

JOHN BANNISTER TABB
1845-1909

COMMUNION

ONCE when my heart was passion-free
    To learn of things divine,
The soul of nature suddenly
    Outpoured itself in mine.

I held the secrets of the deep,
    And of the heavens above;
I knew the harmonies of sleep,
    The mysteries of love.

And for a moment's interval
    The earth, the sky, the sea—
My soul encompassed each and all,
    As now they compass me.

COMMUNION

To one in all, to all in one—

Since Love the work began—

Life's ever widening circles run.

Revealing God and man.

JOHN BANNISTER TABB
1845-1909

ALTER EGO

THOU art to me as is the sea
Unto the shell;
A life whereof I breathe, a love
Wherein I dwell.

JOHN BANNISTER TABB
1845-1909

BETHLEHEM-TOWN

AS I was going to Bethlehem-town,
Upon the earth I cast me down
All underneath a little tree,
That whispered in this wise to me:
"Oh, I shall stand on Calvary
And bear what burthen saveth thee!"

As up I fared to Bethlehem-town,
I met a shepherd coming down
And thus he quoth: "A wondrous sight
Hath spread before mine eyes this night—
An angel host, most fair to see,
That sung full sweetly of a tree
That shall uplift on Calvary
What burthen saveth you and me!"

And as I gat to Bethlehem-town,

Lo! wise men came that bore a crown.

"Is there," cried I, "in Bethlehem

A King shall wear this diadem?"

"Good sooth," they quoth, "and it is He

That shall be lifted on the tree,

And freely shed on Calvary

What blood redeemeth us and thee!"

Unto a Child in Bethlehem-town

The wise men came and brought the crown;

And while the Infant smiling slept,

Upon their knees they fell and wept;

But, with her Babe upon her knee,

Naught recked that Mother of the tree

That should uplift on Calvary

What burthen saveth all and me.

BETHLEHEM-TOWN

Again I walk in Bethlehem-town,

And think on Him that wears the crown.

I may not kiss His feet again,

Nor worship Him as did I then;

My King hath died upon the tree,

And hath outpoured on Calvary

What blood redeemeth you and me!

EUGENE FIELD
1850-1896

COMPANIONSHIP

NO distant Lord have I,
　　Loving afar to be.
Made flesh for me he cannot rest
　　Until he rests in me.

I need not journey far
　　This dearest friend to see.
Companionship is always mine;
　　He makes his home with me.

I envy not the twelve.
　　Nearer to me is he.
The life he once lived here on earth
　　He lives again in me.

COMPANIONSHIP

Ascended now to God
　My witness there to be,
His witness here am I because
　His Spirit dwells in me.

O glorious Son of God,
　Incarnate Deity,
I shall forever be with Thee
　Because Thou art with me.

MALTBIE DAVENPORT BABCOCK
1858-1901

DEO OPTIMO MAXIMO

ALL else for use, One only for desire;
Thanksgiving for the good, but thirst for
Thee:
Up from the best, whereof no man need tire,
Impel Thou me.

Delight is menace, if Thou brood not by,
Power a quicksand, Fame a gathering jeer.
Oft as the morn (though none of earth deny
These three are dear),

Wash me of them, that I may be renewed,
And wander free amid my freeborn joys:
Oh, close my hands upon Beatitude!
Not on her toys.

LOUISE IMOGEN GUINEY
1861-1920

SANCTUARY

HIGH above hate I dwell:
　　O storms! farewell.

Though at my sill your daggered thunders play

Lawless and loud to-morrow as to-day,

To me they sound more small

Than a young fay's footfall;

Soft and far-sunken, forty fathoms low

In Long Ago,

And winnowed into silence on that wind

Which takes wars like a dust, and leaves but
　　love behind.

Hither Felicity

Doth climb to me,

And bank me in with turf and marjoram

Such as bees lip, or the new-weanèd lamb;

With golden barberry wreath,

And bluets thick beneath;

One grosbeak, too, mid apple-buds a guest

With bud-red breast,

Is singing, singing. All the hells that rage

Float less than April fog below our hermitage.

LOUISE IMOGEN GUINEY
1861-1920

TRANSCENDENCE

THOUGH one with all that sense or soul
  can see,
Not imprisoned in his own creations, he;
His life is more than stars or wind or angels—
The sun does not contain him nor the sea.

RICHARD HOVEY
1864-1900

From SPRING

AND do I not hear
The first low stirring of that greater
spring

Thrill in the underworld of the cosmic year?

The wafture of scant violets presaging

The roses and the tasseled corn to be;

A yearning in the roots of grass and trees.

A swallow in the eaves;

The signals of the summer coming up from Arcadie.

For surely, in the blind deep-buried roots

Of all men's souls to-day

A secret quiver shoots.

SPRING

An underground compulsion of new birth

Lays hold upon the dark core of our being.

And unborn blossoms urge their uncomprehended

    way

Toward the outer day.

Unconscious, dumb, unseeing,

The darkness in us is aware

Of something potent burning through the earth,

Of something vital in the procreant air.

Is it a spring, indeed?

Or do we mutter in our dreams,

Only to sleep again?

What warrant have we that we give not heed

To the caprices of an idle brain

That in its slumber deems

The world of slumber real as it seems?

No—

Spring's not to be mistaken.

When her first far flute notes blow

Across the snow,

Bird, beast and blossom know

That she is there.

The very bats awaken

That hang in clusters in Kentucky caves

All winter, breathless, motionless, asleep,

And feel no alteration of the air,

For all year long those vasty caverns keep

Winter and summer, even temperature;

And yet when April whistles on the hill,

Somehow, far in those subterranean naves,

They know, they hear her, they obey her will,

And wake and circle through the vaulted aisles

To find her in the open where she smiles.

So we are somehow sure,

SPRING

By this dumb turmoil in the soul of man,

Of an impending something. When the stress

Climbs to fruition, we can only guess

What many-seeded harvest we shall scan;

But from one impulse, like a northering sun,

The innumerable outburst is begun,

And in that common sunlight all men know

A common ecstasy

And feel themselves at one.

That comradeship of joy and mystery

Thrills us more vitally as we arouse,

And we shall find our new day intimate

Beyond the guess of any long ago.

RICHARD HOVEY
1864-1900

PANDORA'S SONG
From THE FIRE-BRINGER

I STOOD within the heart of God;
  It seemed a place that I had known:
(I was blood-sister to the clod,
  Blood-brother to the stone.)

I found my love and labor there,
  My house, my raiment, meat and wine,
My ancient rage, my old despair,—
  Yea, all things that were mine.

I saw the spring and summer pass,
  The trees grow bare, and winter come;
All was the same as once it was
  Upon my hills at home.

PANDORA'S SONG

Then suddenly in my own heart
    I felt God walk and gaze about;
He spoke; His words seemed held apart
    With gladness and with doubt.

"Here is my meat and wine," He said,
    "My love, my toil, my ancient care;
Here is my cloak, my book, my bed,
    And here my old despair;

"Here are my seasons: winter, spring,
    Summer the same, and autumn spills
The fruits I look for; everything
    As on my heavenly hills."

WILLIAM VAUGHN MOODY
1869-1910

GOOD FRIDAY NIGHT

A T last the bird that sang so long
  In twilight circles, hushed his song:
Above the ancient square
The stars came here and there.

Good Friday night! Some hearts were bowed,
But some amid the waiting crowd
Because of too much youth
Felt not the mystic ruth;

And of these hearts my heart was one:
Nor when beneath the arch of stone
With dirge and candle flame
The cross of passion came,

GOOD FRIDAY NIGHT

Did my glad spirit feel reproof,
Though on the awful tree aloof,
Unspiritual, dead,
Drooped the ensanguined Head.

To one who stood where myrtles made
A little space of deeper shade
(As I could half descry
A stranger, even as I),

I said, "These youths who bear along
The symbols of their Saviour's wrong,
The spear, the garment torn,
The flaggel, and the thorn,—

"Why do they make this mummery?
Would not a brave man gladly die
For a much smaller thing
Than to be Christ and king?"

He answered nothing, and I turned.

Throned in its hundred candles burned

The jeweled eidolon

Of her who bore the Son.

The crowd was prostrate; still, I felt

No shame until the stranger knelt;

Then not to kneel, almost

Seemed like a vulgar boast.

I knelt.   The doll-face, waxen white,

Flowered out a living dimness; bright

Dawned the dear mortal grace

Of my own mother's face.

When we were risen up, the street

Was vacant; all the air hung sweet

With lemon-flowers; and soon

The sky would hold the moon.

GOOD FRIDAY NIGHT

More silently than new-found friends
To whom much silence makes amends
For the much babble vain
While yet their lives were twain,

We walked along the odorous hill.
The light was little yet; his will
I could not see to trace
Upon his form or face.

So when aloft the gold moon broke,
I cried, heart-stung. As one who woke
He turned unto my cries
The anguish of his eyes.

"Friend! Master!" I cried falteringly,
"Thou seest the thing they make of thee.
 Oh, by the light divine
 My mother shares with thine,

121

"I beg that I may lay my head
Upon thy shoulder and be fed
With thoughts of brotherhood!"
So through the odorous wood,

More silently than friends new-found
We walked. At the first meadow bound
His figure ashen-stoled
Sank in the moon's broad gold.

WILLIAM VAUGHN MOODY
1869-1910

From JETSAM

ONCE at a simple turning of the way
    I met God walking; and although the
    dawn
Was large behind Him, and the morning stars
Circled and sang about his face as birds
About the fieldward morning cottager,
My coward heart said faintly, "Let us haste!
Day grows and it is far to market-town."
Once where I lay in darkness after fight,
Sore smitten, thrilled a little thread of song
Searching and searching all my muffled sense
Until it shook sweet pangs through all my blood,
And I beheld one globed in ghostly fire

Singing, star-strong, her golden canticle;

And her mouth sang, "The hosts of Hate roll
past,

A dance of dust-motes in the sliding sun;

Love's battle comes on the wide wings of storm,

From east to west one legion! Wilt thou strive?"

Then, since the splendor of her sword-bright
gaze

Was heavy on me with yearning and with scorn,

My sick heart muttered, "Yea, the little strife,

Yet see, the grievous wounds! I fain would
sleep."

O heart, shalt thou not once be strong to go

Where all sweet throats are calling, once be brave

To slake with deed thy dumbness? Let us go

The path her singing face looms low to point,

JETSAM

Pendulous, blanched with longing, shedding
    flames
Of silver on the brown grope of the flood;
For all my spirit's soilure is put by
And all my body's soilure, lacking now
But the last lustral sacrament of death
To make me clean for those near-searching eyes
That question yonder whether all be well,
And pause a little ere they dare rejoice.

Question and be thou answered, passionate face!
For I am worthy, worthy now at last
After so long unworth; strong now at last
To give myself to beauty and be saved.

WILLIAM VAUGHN MOODY
1869-1910

AFTER MUSIC

I SAW not they were strange, the ways I
roam,
  Until the music called, and called me thence,
And tears stirred in my heart as tears may come
To lonely children straying far from home,
    Who know not how they wandered so, nor
    whence.

If I might follow far and far away
  Unto that country where these songs abide,
I think my soul would wake and find it day,
Would tell me who I am, and why I stray,—
    Would tell me who I was before I died.

JOSEPHINE PRESTON PEABODY
1874-1922

IN THE SILENCE

WHERE did'st thou tarry, Lord, Lor
    Who heeded not my prayer?
All the long day, all the long night,
  I stretched my hands to air.

"There was a bitterer want than thine
    Came from the frozen North;
Laid hands upon my garment's hem
    And led me forth.

"It was a lonely Northern man,
    Where there was never tree
To shed its comfort on his heart,
    There he had need of me.

"He kindled us a little flame
    To hope against the storm;
And unto him, and unto me,
    The light was warm."

And yet I called Thee, Lord, Lord—
    Who answered not, nor came:
All the long day, and yesterday,
    I called Thee by Thy name.

"There was a dumb, unhearing grief
    Spake louder than thy word,
There was a heart called not on me
    And yet I heard.

"The sorrow of a savage man
    Shaping him gods, alone,
Who found no love in the shapen clay
    To answer to his own.

IN THE SILENCE

"His heart knew what his eyes saw not;
    He bade me stay and eat;
  And unto him, and unto me,
    The cup was sweet.

"Too long we wait for thee and thine,
    In sodden ways and dim,
  And where the man's need cries on me
    There have I need of him.

"Along the borders of despair
    Where sparrows seek no nest,
  Nor ravens food, I sit at meat—
    The Unnamed Guest."

JOSEPHINE PRESTON PEABODY
1874-1922

PENETRALIA *

I AM a part of all you see
    In Nature; part of all you feel;
I am the impact of the bee
Upon the blossom; in the tree
I am the sap—that shall reveal
The leaf, the bloom—that flows and flutes
Up from the darkness through its roots.

I am the vermeil of the rose,
The perfume breathing in its veins;
The gold within the mist that glows
Along the west and overflows
With light the heaven; the dew that rains

---

* By permission from *Poems* by Madison Cawein, copyright by The Macmillan Company.

PENETRALIA

Its freshness down and strings with spheres
Of wet the webs and oaten ears.

I am the egg that folds the bird;
The song that beaks and breaks its shell;
The laughter and the wandering word
The water says; and, dimly heard,
The music of the blossom's bell
When soft winds swing it; and the sound
Of grass slow-creeping o'er the ground.

I am the warmth, the honey-scent
That throats with spice each lily-bud
That opens, white with wonderment,
Beneath the moon; or, downward bent,
Sleeps with a moth beneath its hood:
I am the dream that haunts it too,
That crystallizes into dew.

131

AMERICAN MYSTICAL VERSE

I am the seed within the pod;

The worm within its closed cocoon:

The wings within the circling clod,

The germ that gropes through soil and sod

To beauty, radiant in the noon:

I am all these, behold! and more—

I am the love at the world-heart's core.

MADISON JULIUS CAWEIN
1865-1914

THE PEAKS

IN the night
   Gray, heavy clouds muffled the valleys
And the peaks looked toward God alone;
   "O Master, that moveth the wind with a finger,
   Humble, idle, futile peaks are we.
   Grant that we may run swiftly across the
      world
   To huddle in worship at Thy feet."

In the morning
A noise of men at work came through the clear
      blue miles,
And the little black cities were apparent.
   "O Master, that knowest the meaning of rain-
      drops,

Humble, idle, futile peaks are we.

Give voice to us, we pray, O Lord,

That we may sing Thy goodness to the sun."

In the evening

The far valleys were sprinkled with tiny lights.

"O Master,

Thou that knowest the value of kings and
birds,

Thou hast made us humble, idle, futile peaks.

Thou only needest eternal patience;

We bow to Thy wisdom, O Lord—

Humble, idle, futile peaks."

In the night

Gray, heavy clouds muffled the valleys,

And the peaks looked toward God alone.

STEPHEN CRANE
1870-1900

134

HYMN

O LI'L' lamb out in de col',
  De Mastah call you to de fol',
    O li'l' lamb!
He hyeah you bleatin' on de hill;
Come hyeah an' keep yo' mou'nin' still,
    O li'l' lamb!

De Mastah send de Shepud fo'f;
He wandah souf, he wandah no'f,
    O li'l' lamb!
He wandah eas', he wandah wes';
De win' a-wrenchin' at his breas',
    O li'l' lamb!

135

Oh, tell de Shepud whaih you hide;

He want you walkin' by his side,

> O li'l' lamb!

He know you weak, he know you so';

But come, don' stay away no mo';

> O li'l' lamb!

An' af' ah while de lamb he hyeah

De Shepud's voice a-callin' cleah—

> Sweet li'l' lamb!

He answah f'om de brambles thick,

"O Shepud, I's a-comin' quick"—

> O li'l' lamb!

PAUL LAWRENCE DUNBAR
1872-1906

SOMEWHERE I KNOW

SOMEWHERE, I know, the sky at this
bright hour
Is brighter than the long flash of the seas
Flung in a mellow curve against the breeze;
Somewhere, I know, one frail and wistful flower
Breathes to my heart more of the magic power
And pain of loveliness than all the trees
That shower ripe light on a thousand Hesperides
Leaving the stars ecstatic with the shower.

Somewhere, I know, there is an island's link
Of splendor beat and braided to the moon
Like blossom to blossom in an eternal June;

Somewhere, I know, there shines for me the brink

Of ultimate beauty, and may I thither climb

On the pale ladder of one immortal rhyme.

JOSEPH AUSLANDER

CONCERT PITCH

TAKE then the music, plunge in the
thickest of it,
Thickest, darkest, richest: call it a forest,
A million boles of trees, with leaves, leaves,
Golden and green, flashing like scales in the sun,
Tossed and torn in the tempest, whirling and
streaming,
With the terrible sound beneath, of boughs that
crack . . . .
Again, a hush comes; and the wind's a whisper.
One leaf gone pirouetting. You stand in the
dusk,
In the misty shaft of light the sun flings faintly

Through planes of green and suddenly, out of the
darkest

And deepest and farthest of the forest, wavers

That golden horn, cor anglais, husky-timbred,

Sending through all that gloom of trees and
silence

Its faint half-mute nostalgia. . . . How the soul

Flies from the dungeon of you to the very portals

To meet that sound! There, there is the secret

Singing out of the darkness—shining, too,

For all we know, if we could only see! . . .

But if we steal by footpaths, warily—

Snap not a twig, nor crush a single leaf;

Or if, in a kind of panic, like wild beasts,

We rend our headlong way through vines and
briars,

CONCERT PITCH

We crash through a coppice, tear our flesh, come
    bleeding
To a still pool, encircled, brooded over
By ancient trees—all's one! We reach but
    silence,
We find no horn, no hornsman. . . . There the
    beeches
Out of the lower dark of ferns and mosses
Lift far above their tremulous tops to the light.
Only an echo have we of that horn,
Anglais, golden, husky-timbred, crying
Half-mute nostalgia from the dusk of things . . .
Then, as we stand bewildered in that wood,
With leaves above us in sibilant confusion,
And the ancient ghosts of leaves about our feet—
Listen!—the horn once more, but farther now,
Sings in the evening for a wing-beat space;

Makes the leaves murmur, as it makes the blood

Burn in the heart and all its radiant veins;

And we turn inward, to seek it once again.

Or, it's morning in the blue portal of summer.

White shoals of little clouds, like heavenly fish,

Swim softly off the sun, who rains his light

On the vast hurrying earth. The giant poplar

Sings in the light with a thousand sensitive leaves,

Root-tip to leaf-tip he is all delight:

And, at the golden core of all that joy,

One sinister grackle with a thievish eye

Scrapes a harsh cynic comment. How he laughs,

Flaunting amid that green his coffin color!

We, in the garden, a million miles below him,

At paltry tasks of pruning, spading, watching

Blade-striped bees crawl into foxglove bells

Half-filled with dew—look! we are lightly startled

CONCERT PITCH

By sense or sound: are moved; lose touch with
    earth:
And, in the twinkling of a grackle's eye,
Swing in the infinite on a spider's cable.
What is our world? It is a poplar tree
Immense and solitary, with leaves a thousand,
Or million, countless, flashing in a light
For them alone intended. He is great,
His trunk is solid, and his roots deceive us.
We shade our eyes with hands, and upward look
To see if all those leaves indeed be leaves—
So rich they are in a choiring down of joy—
Or stars. And as we stand so, small and dumb,
We hear again that harsh derisive comment,
The grackle's laughter; and again we see
His thievish eye, aware amid green boughs. . . .
Touch earth again, take up your shovel, dig

AMERICAN MYSTICAL VERSE

In the wormy ground! That tree magnificent
Sways like a giant dancer in a garment
Whose gold and green are naught but tricks of
 light
And at the heart of all that drunken beauty
Is a small lively cynic bird who laughs.

Who sees the vision coming? Who can tell
What moment out of time will be the seed
To root itself, as swift as lightning roots
Into a cloud, and grow, swifter than thought,
And flower gigantic in the infinite? . . .
Walk softly through your forest, and be ready
To hear the horn of horns. Or in your garden
Stoop, but upon your back be ever conscious
Of sunlight, and a shadow that may grow.

CONRAD AIKEN

THE FALCONER OF GOD

I FLUNG my soul to the air like a falcon
flying.
I said, "Wait on, wait on, while I ride below!
I shall start a heron soon
In the marsh beneath the moon—
A strange white heron rising with silver on its
wings,
Rising and crying
Wordless, wondrous things;
The secret of the stars, of the world's heart-
strings,
The answer to their woe.
Then stoop thou upon him, and grip and hold him
so!"

My wild soul waited on as falcons hover.

I beat the reedy fens as I trampled past.

> I heard the mournful loon
>
> In the marsh beneath the moon.

And then—with feathery thunder—the bird of my
    desire

> > Broke from the cover
> >
> Flashing silver fire.

High up among the stars I saw his pinions spire.

> The pale clouds gazed aghast

As my falcon stoopt upon him, and gript and held
    him fast.

My soul dropt through the air—with heavenly
    plunder?—

Gripping the dazzling bird my dreaming knew?

> Nay! but a piteous freight,
>
> A dark and heavy weight

THE FALCONER OF GOD

Despoiled of silver plumage, its voice forever
    stilled—
        All of the wonder
      Gone that ever filled
Its guise with glory. Oh, bird that I have killed,
      How brilliantly you flew
Across my rapturous vision when first I dreamed
    of you!

Yet I fling my soul on high with new endeavor,
And I ride the world below with a joyful mind.
      I shall start a heron soon
      In the marsh beneath the moon—
A wondrous silver heron its inner darkness
    fledges!
        I beat forever
      The fens and the sedges.

147

AMERICAN MYSTICAL VERSE

The pledge is still the same—for all disastrous
  pledges,

   All hopes resigned!

My soul still flies above me for the quarry it shall
  find.

WILLIAM ROSE BENÉT

THE MONK IN THE KITCHEN

I

O RDER is a lovely thing;
⠀⠀⠀On disarray it lays its wing,
Teaching simplicity to sing.

It has a meek and lowly grace,

Quiet as a nun's face.

Lo—I will have thee in this place!

Tranquil well of deep delight,

Transparent as the water, bright—

All things that shine through thee appear

As stones through water, sweetly clear.

Thou clarity,

That with angelic charity

Revealest beauty where thou art,

Spread thyself like a clean pool.

Then all the things that in thee are,

Shall seem more spiritual and fair,

Reflections from serener air—

Sunken shapes of many a star

In the high heavens set afar.

II

Ye stolid, homely, visible things,

Above you all brood glorious wings

Of your deep entities, set high,

Like slow moons in a hidden sky.

But you, their likenesses, are spent

Upon another element.

Truly ye are but seemings—

The shadowy cast-off gleamings

Of bright solidities. Ye seem

Soft as water, vague as dream;

Image, cast in a shifting stream.

THE MONK IN THE KITCHEN

III

What are ye?

I know not.

Brazen pan and iron pot,

Yellow brick and gray flagstone

That my feet have trod upon—

Ye seem to me

Vessels of bright mystery.

For ye do bear a shape, and so

Though ye were made by man, I know

An inner Spirit also made

And ye his breathings have obeyed.

IV

Shape, the strong and awful Spirit,

Laid his ancient hand on you.

He waste chaos doth inherit;

He can alter and subdue.

AMERICAN MYSTICAL VERSE

Verily, he doth lift up
Matter, like a sacred cup.
Into deep substance he reached, and lo
Where ye were not, ye were; and so
Out of useless nothing, ye
Groaned and laughed and came to be.
And I use you, as I can,
Wonderful uses, made for man,
Iron pot and brazen pan.

V

What are ye?
I know not;
Nor what I really do
When I move and govern you.
There is no small work unto God.
He requires of us greatness;

THE MONK IN THE KITCHEN

Of His least creature

A high angelic nature,

Stature superb and bright completeness.

He sets to us no humble duty.

Each act that He would have us do

Is haloed round with strangest beauty.

Terrific deeds and cosmic tasks

Of His plainest child He asks.

When I polish the brazen pan

I hear a creature laugh afar

In the gardens of a star,

And from His burning presence run

Flaming wheels of many a sun.

Whoever makes a thing more bright,

He is an angel of all light.

When I cleanse this earthen floor

My spirit leaps to see

Bright garments trailing over it.

Wonderful lustres cover it,

A cleanness made by me.

Purger of all men's thoughts and ways,

With labor do I sound Thy praise,

My work is done for Thee.

Whoever makes a thing more bright,

He is an angel of all light.

Therefore let me spread abroad

The beautiful cleanness of my God.

VI

One time in the cool of dawn

Angels came and worked with me.

The air was soft with many a wing,

They laughed amid my solitude

And cast bright looks on everything.

Sweetly of me did they ask

THE MONK IN THE KITCHEN

That they might do my common task.

And all were beautiful—but one

With garments whiter than the sun

Had such a face

Of deep, remembered grace,

That when I saw I cried—"Thou art

The great Blood-Brother of my heart.

Where have I seen thee?"—And he said,

"When we are dancing 'round God's throne,

How often thou art there.

Beauties from thy hands have flown

Like white doves wheeling in mid air.

Nay—thy soul remembers not?

Work on, and cleanse thy iron pot."

VII

What are we?   I know not.

ANNA HEMPSTEAD BRANCH

155

DREAM

BUT now the Dream has come again, the
world is as of old.

Once more I feel about my breast the heartening
splendors fold.

Now I am back in that good place from which
my footsteps came,

And I am hushed of any grief and have laid by
my shame.

I know not by what road I came—oh wonderful
and fair!

Only I know I ailed for thee and that thou wert
not there.

DREAM

Then suddenly Time's stalwart wall before thee
 did divide,
Its solid bastions dreamed and swayed and there
 was I inside.

It is thy nearness makes thee seem so wonderful
 and far.
In that deep sky thou art obscured as in the noon,
 a star.
But when the darkness of my grief swings up
 the mid-day sky,
My need begets a shining world. Lo, in thy light
 am I.

All that I used to be is there and all I yet shall be.
My laughter deepens in the air, my quiet in the
 tree.

My utter tremblings of delight are manna from
the sky,

And shining flower-like in the grass my inno-
cencies lie.

And here I run and sleep and laugh and have no
name at all.

Only if God should speak to me then I would
heed the call.

And I forget the curious ways, the alien looks of
men,

For even as it was of old, so is it now again.

Still every angel looks the same and all the folks
are there

That are so bounteous and mild and have not any
care.

DREAM

But kindest to me is the one I would most choose
to be.

She is so beautiful and sheds such loving looks
on me.

She is so beautiful—and lays her cheek against
my own.

Back—in the world—they all will say, "How
happy you have grown."

Her breath is sweet about my eyes and she has
healed me now,

Though I be scarred with grief, I keep her kiss
upon my brow.

All day, sweet land, I fight for thee outside the
goodly wall,

And 'twixt my breathless wounds I have no sight
of thee at all!

And sometimes I forget thy looks and what thy
ways may be!

I have denied thou wert at all—yet still I fight
for thee.

ANNA HEMPSTEAD BRANCH

HORA CHRISTI *

SWEET is the time for joyous folk
   Of gifts and minstrelsy;
Yet I, O lowly-hearted One,
   Crave but Thy company.
On lonesome road, beset with dread,
   My questing lies afar.
I have no light, save in the east
   The gleaming of Thy star.

In cloistered aisles they keep to-day
   Thy feast, O living Lord!
With pomp of banner, pride of song,

* By permission from *The Road to Castally* by Alice
Brown, copyright, 1917, by The Macmillan Company.

And stately sounding word.
Mute stand the kings of power and place,
  While priests of holy mind
Dispense Thy blessed heritage
  Of peace to all mankind.

I know a spot where budless twigs
  Are bare above the snow,
And where sweet winter-loving birds
  Flit softly to and fro;
There, with the sun for altar-fire,
  The earth for kneeling-place,
The gentle air for chorister,
  Will I adore Thy face.

Lord, underneath the great blue sky,
  My heart shall pæan sing,
The gold and myrrh of meekest love

HORA CHRISTI

Mine only offering.

Bliss of Thy birth shall quicken me,

    And for Thy pain and dole

Tears are but vain, so I will keep

    The silence of the soul.

ALICE BROWN

QUO VADIS?

FARE not abroad, O Soul, to win
　　Man's friendly smile or favoring nod;
Be still, be strong, and seek within
　　The Comradeship of God.

Beyond is not the journey's end,
　　The fool goes wayfaring apart,
And even as he goes his Friend
　　Is knocking at his heart.

MYLES E. CONNOLLY

THE SEARCH

NO one could tell me where my Soul might
be.

I searched for God, but God eluded me.

I sought my Brother out, and found all three.

ERNEST HOWARD CROSBY

PROFITS *

YES, stars were with me formerly.
(I also knew the wind and sea;
And hilltops had my feet by heart.
Their shagged heights would sting and start
When I came leaping on their backs.
I knew the earth's queer crooked cracks,
Where hidden waters weave a low
And druid chant of joy and woe.)

But stars were with me most of all.
I heard them flame and break and fall.
Their excellent array, their free
Encounter with Eternity,

* By permission from *Crack o' Dawn* by Fannie Stearns Davis, copyright, 1915, by The Macmillan Company.

PROFITS

I learned. And it was good to know
That where God walked, I too might go.
Now all these things are passed. For I
Grow very old and glad to die.
What did they profit me, say you,
These distant bloodless things I knew?

Profit? What profit hath the sea
Of her deep-throated threnody?
What profit hath the sun, who stands
Staring on space with idle hands?
And what should God himself acquire
From all the æons' blood and fire?

My profit is as theirs: to be
Made proof against mortality:
To know that I have companied
With all that shines and lives, amid

AMERICAN MYSTICAL VERSE

So much the years sift through their hands,

Most mortal, windy, worthless sands.

This day I have great peace. With me

Shall stars abide eternally!

FANNIE STEARNS DAVIS

THE COMRADE

CALL me friend or foe,
  Little I care!
I go with all who go
  Daring to dare.

I am the force,
  I am the fire,
I am the secret source
  Of desire.

I am the urge,
  The spur and thong;
Moon of the tides that surge
  Into song!

AMERICAN MYSTICAL VERSE

Call me friend or foe,
 Little care I,
I go with all who go
 Singing to die.

Call me friend or foe. . . .
 Taking to give,
I go with all who go
 Dying to live

LEE WILSON DODD

THE SECRET WAY *

STARK on the window's early gray
  Lined out in squares by casement bars,
She saw her lily lift to take
  The sinking stars.

Within the room's delaying dark
  Intimate things lay dim and still
With all their daytime friendliness
  Gone false and chill.

Her hand upon the coverlet,
  Her face low in the linen's cleft,
They were as wan as water-flowers
  By light bereft.

* By permission from *The Secret Way* by Zona Gale, copyright, 1921, by The Macmillan Company.

And never was bloom brought to her couch
　　But shed the odor of a sigh
Because she was as white as they,
　　And they must die.

"O Pale, lit deep within the dark
　　Of your young eyes, a stifled light
Leaps thin and keen as melody
　　And leavens night.

"It is a light that did not burn
　　When you were gay at mart and fair;
O Pale, what is that starry fire,
　　Fed unaware?"

Then softly she: "I may not tell
　　What other eyes behold in mine;
But I have melted night and day
　　In some wild wine.

THE SECRET WAY

"I may not read the graven cup
  Exhaustless as a brimming bell
Distilling silver; but I drank
  And all is well.

"One morn like this, bitter still,
  I waited for the early stir
Of those who slept the while I watched
  What muffled wonders were.

"I saw my lily on the sill;
  I saw my mirror on the wall
Take light that was not; and I saw
  My spectral taper tall.

"Why, I had known these quiet things
  Since I could speak. Yet suddenly
They all touched hands and in one breath
  They spoke to me.

"I may not tell you what they said.
  The strange part is that I must lie
And never tell you what we say—
  These things and I.

"I only know that common things
  Bear sudden little spirits set
Free by the rose of dawn and by
  Night's violet.

"I only know that when I hear
  Clear tone, the haunted echoes bear
Legions of little winged feet
  On printless air.

"And when warm color weds my look
  A word is uttered tremblingly,
With meaning full—but I know not
  What it may be.

THE SECRET WAY

"I only know that now I find
　　Abiding beauty everywhere;
Or if it bide not, that it fades
　　Is still more fair.

"I long to question those I love
　　And yet I know not what to say;
I am alone as one upon
　　Some secret way.

"My words are barren of my bliss;
　　The strange part is that I must lie
And never tell you what we say—
　　These things and I.

"So will it be when I am not.
　　A little more perhaps to tell;
Yet then as now I may not say
　　What I know well."

AMERICAN MYSTICAL VERSE

She died when all the east was red.

And we are they who know her fate
Because we love the way of life
That she had found too late.

Zona Gale

CONTOURS *

I AM glad of the straight lines of the rain;
   Of the free blowing curves of the grain;

Of the perilous swirling and curling of fire;

The sharp upthrust of a spire;

Of the ripples on the river

Where the patterns curl and quiver

And sun thrills;

Of the innumerable undulations of the hills.

But the true line is drawn from my spirit to some

   infinite outward place . . .

That line I cannot trace.

Zona Gale

---

* By permission from *The Secret Way* by Zona Gale, copyright, 1921, by The Macmillan Company.

LIGHT *

WE do not touch the texture of the light.
But one may see with a secret eye
The things that are.

Then we divine that we need not die

To win our heritage of sight.

As well this earth as any other star.

Waking from dream there trails an alien air,

A residue of other suns than these;

We know that we have walked an inner way,

Have met familiars there

And kept our step in exquisite concord

* By permission from *The Secret Way* by Zona Gale,. copyright, 1921, by The Macmillan Company.

LIGHT

The while we spoke some unremembered word.

And over all there lay

Light whose vibrations ran to other keys

Than those we woke upon. Light whose long play

Was dappled color delicately kissed.

Strange fires rayed from strange regions of the
Lord.

Light from the sun behind the sun fell where

We went to keep our tryst.

In sleep and in the solitary dusk there come

Fine lines of light upon the lowered lids,

A flush that lets us in the heart of night

And hints dear wonders to be there at home;

As if the universal fabric bids

Its human pattern know that all is light.

In snow

Have we not seen the whiteness smitten through

AMERICAN MYSTICAL VERSE

With sudden rays of glory, vague with veils,

Of some beloved hue that pales

To earthly rose and violet and blue?

Oh you

Who pulse within that light—we know, we know!

Soon

From without transition night

We would come into this, our own.

Then the dim tune

The which we almost hear,

The low-keyed color and the word

We have not heard,

All these we shall be shown,

And infinitely near

To God, breathe for our breath his light.

Zona Gale

HALF THOUGHT *

I CLOSE my eyes and on the night
    A face looks in at me.
It speaks a word like burning light;
I answer joyfully.
It dims away.   The word is sped.
I know not what we two have said.

The old dark sparkles like a star.
And when shall we be touched with sight
To find the things that are?

ZONA GALE

---

* By permission from *The Secret Way* by Zona Gale, copyright, 1921, by The Macmillan Company.

DE SHEEPFOL'

DE massa ob de sheepfol',
　　Dat guards de sheepfol' bin,
Look out in de gloomerin' meadows,
Wha'r de long night rain begin—
So he call to de hirelin' shepa'd,
"Is my sheep, is dey all come in?
My sheep, is dey all come in?"

Oh, den, says de hirelin' shepa'd:
"Dey's some, dey's black and thin,
And some, dey's po' ol' wedda's,
Dat can't come home agin.
Dey's some black sheep an' ol' wedda's,
But de res', dey's all brung in.—
De res', dey's all brung in."

DE SHEEPFOL

Den de massa ob de sheepfol',

Dat guards de sheepfol' bin,

Goes down in de gloomerin' meadows,

Wha'r de long night rain begin—

So he le' down de ba's ob de sheepfol',

Callin' sof', "Come in.   Come in."

Callin' sof', "Come in. Come in."

Den up t'ro' de gloomerin' meadows,

T'ro' de col' night rain and win',

And up t'ro' de gloomerin' rain-paf',

Wha'r de sleet fa' pie'cin', thin,

De po' los' sheep ob de sheepfol',

Dey all comes gadderin' in.

De po' los' sheep ob de sheepfol',

Dey all comes gadderin' in.

SARAH PRATT McLEAN GREENE

THE THIN DOOR

WHEN you have walked where you would
walk,

And tired your feet of streets and lanes,

Behind a thin door you will talk

Of what you know of suns or rains.

Much you will tell of cooling fact.

You will name the hours dawn and noon,

Predict how all the stars will act,

And where the sky will wear the moon.

Yet there will be what you cannot say

Hardened in thought, as in a mine

Lies the unlighted ore; to-day

Has held more than you can define.

THE THIN DOOR

What you may tell is the desperate reach

Of tongues now satiate with clay,

And what will glitter beyond your speech

Is what an unshaped tongue will say.

HAZEL HALL

SUNLIGHT THROUGH A WINDOW

BEAUTY streamed into my hand,
    In sunlight through a pane of glass;
Now at last I understand
Why suns must pass.

I have held a shadow, cool
Reflection of a burning gold,
And it has been more beautiful
Than hands should hold.

To that delicate tracery
Of light, a force my lips must name
In whispers of uncertainty,
Has answered through me in a flame.

186

SUNLIGHT THROUGH A WINDOW

Beauty is a core of fire

To reaching hands; even its far

Passing leaves a hurt desire

Like a scar.

HAZEL HALL

FLASH

I AM less of myself and more of the sun
　　The beat of life is wearing me
To an incomplete oblivion,
Yet not to the certain dignity
Of death. *They cannot even die*
Who have not lived. . . .

　　　　The hungry jaws
Of space snap at my unlearned eye, ʻ
And time tears in my flesh like claws.

If I am not life's, if I am not death's,
Out of chaos I must re-reap
The burden of untasted breaths.
Who has not wakened may not yet sleep.

Hazel Hall

THE INDWELLING GOD

O that I knew where I might find Him.

GO not, my soul, in search of Him;
  Thou wilt not find Him there—
Or in the depths of shadows dim,
  Or heights of upper air.

For not in far-off realms of space
  The Spirit hath its throne;
In every heart it findeth place
  And waiteth to be known.

Thought answereth alone to thought,
  And soul with soul hath kin;
The outward God he findeth not,
  Who finds not God within.

And if the vision come to thee
  Revealed by inward sign,
Earth will be full of Deity
  And with His glory shine!

Thou shalt not want for company,
  Nor pitch thy tent alone;
The indwelling God will go with thee,
  And show thee of His own.

O gift of gifts, O grace of grace,
  That God should condescend
To make thy heart His dwelling place—
  And be thy daily friend!

Then go not thou in search of Him,
  But to thyself repair;
Wait thou within the silence dim,
  And thou shalt find Him there.

FREDERICK LUCIAN HOSMER

JOYOUS-GARD

WIND-WASHED and free, full-swept by
  rain and wave,
 By tang of surf and thunder of the gale,
 Wild be the ride yet safe the barque will sail
And past the plunging seas her harbor brave;
Nor care have I that storms and waters rave,
 I cannot fear since you can never fail—
 Once have I looked upon the burning grail,
And through your eyes have seen beyond the
  grave.

I know at last—the strange, sweet mystery,
 The nameless joy that trembled into tears,

The hush of wings when you were at my side—

For now the veil is rent and I can see,

See the true vision of the future years,

As in your face the love of Him who died!

THOMAS S. JONES, JR.

IN THE GARDEN OF THE LORD

THE word of God came unto me,
    Sitting alone among the multitudes;
And my blind eyes were touched with light.
And there was laid upon my lips a flame of fire.

I laugh and shout for life is good,
Though my feet are set in silent ways.
In merry mood I leave the crowd
To walk in my garden. Ever as I walk
I gather fruits and flowers in my hands.
And with joyful heart I bless the sun
That kindles all the place with radiant life.
I run with playful winds that blow the scent

Of rose and jessamine in playful whirls.

At last I come where tall lilies grow,

Lifting their faces like white saints to God.

While the lilies pray, I kneel upon the ground;

I have strayed into the holy temple of the Lord.

HELEN KELLER

THE SECOND CRUCIFIXION

LOUD mockers in the roaring street
   Say Christ is crucified again:
Twice pierced His gospel-bearing feet,
   Twice broken His great heart in vain.

I hear, and to myself I smile,
For Christ talks with me all the while.

No angel now to roll the stone
   From off His unawaking sleep.
In vain shall Mary watch alone,
   In vain the soldiers vigil keep.

Yet while they deem my Lord is dead
My eyes are on His shining head.

AMERICAN MYSTICAL VERSE

Ah! nevermore shall Mary hear
  That voice exceeding sweet and low
Within the garden calling clear:
  Her Lord is gone, and she must go.

Yet all the while my Lord I meet
In every London lane and street.

Poor Lazarus shall wait in vain,
  And Bartimæus still go blind;
The healing hem shall ne'er again
  Be touched by suffering humankind.

Yet all the while I see them rest,
The poor and outcast, on His breast.

No more unto the stubborn heart
  With gentle knocking shall He plead,

THE SECOND CRUCIFIXION

No more the mystic pity start,

    For Christ twice dead is dead indeed.

So in the street I hear men say,

Yet Christ is with me all the day.

RICHARD LE GALLIENNE

TO THE VICTOR

MAN'S mind is larger than his brow of
tears;
This hour is not my all of time; this place
My all of earth; nor this obscene disgrace
My all of life; and thy complacent sneers
Shall not pronounce my doom to my compeers
While the Hereafter lights me in the face,
And from the Past, as from the mountain's base,
Rise, as I rise, the long tumultuous cheers.

And who slays me must overcome a world:
Heroes at arms, and virgins who became
Mothers of children, prophecy and song;

TO THE VICTOR

Walls of old cities with their flags unfurled;

Peaks, headlands, ocean and its isles of fame—

And sun and moon and all that made me strong!

WILLIAM ELLERY LEONARD

THE SOUL OF THE CITY RECEIVES THE GIFT OF THE HOLY SPIRIT *

CENSERS are swinging
Over the town;

Censers are swinging,

Look overhead!

Censers are swinging,

Heaven comes down.

City, dead city,

Awake from the dead!

Censers, tremendous,

Gleam overhead.

Wind-harps are ringing,

* By permission from *Collected Poems* by Vachel Lindsay, copyright, 1923, by The Macmillan Company.

THE SOUL OF THE CITY

Wind-harps unseen—

Calling and calling:

"Wake from the dead.

Rise, little city,

Shine like a queen."

Soldiers of Christ

For battle grow keen.

Heaven-sent winds

Haunt alley and lane.

Singing of life

In town meadows green

After the toil

And battle and pain.

Incense is pouring

Like the spring rain

Down on the mob

That moil through the street.

Blessed are they

Who behold it and gain

Power made more mighty

Thro' every defeat.

Builders toil on.

Make all complete.

Make Springfield wonderful.

Make her renown

Worthy this day,

Till, at God's feet

Tranced, saved forever,

Waits the white town.

Censers are swinging

Over the town,

Censers gigantic!

THE SOUL OF THE CITY

Look overhead!

Hear the winds singing:

"Heaven comes down.

City, dead city,

Awake from the dead."

VACHEL LINDSAY

HEART OF GOD *

O GREAT heart of God,
  Once vague and lost to me,
Why do I throb with your throb to-night,
In this land, eternity?

O little heart of God,
Sweet intruding stranger,
You are laughing in my human breast,
A Christ-child in a manger.

Heart, dear heart of God,
Beside you now I kneel,

HEART OF GOD

Strong heart of faith. O heart not mine,

Where God has set His seal.

Wild thundering heart of God

Out of my doubt I come,

And my foolish feet with prophets' feet,

March with the prophets' drum.

VACHEL LINDSAY

THE WHIRLWIND ROAD

THE Muses wrapt in mysteries of light
  Came in a rush of music on the night;
And I was lifted wildly on quick wings,
And borne away into the deep of things.
The dead doors of my being broke apart;
A wind of rapture blew across the heart;
The inward song of worlds rang still and clear;
I felt the Mystery the Muses fear.
Yet they went swiftening on the ways untrod,
And hurled me breathless at the feet of God.

I felt faint touches of the Final Truth—
Moments of trembling love, moments of youth.
A vision swept away the human wall:

206

THE WHIRLWIND ROAD

Slowly I saw the meaning of it all—

Meaning of life and time and death and birth,

But can not tell it to the men of Earth.

I only point the way, and they must go

The whirlwind road of song if they would know.

EDWIN MARKHAM

THE INVISIBLE BRIDE

THE low-voiced girls that go
  In gardens of the Lord,
Like flowers of the field they grow
  In sisterly accord.

Their whispering feet are white
  Along the leafy ways;
They go in whirls of light
  Too beautiful for praise.

And in their band forsooth
  Is one to set me free—
The one that touched my youth—
  The one God gave to me.

208

THE INVISIBLE BRIDE

She kindles the desire
  Whereby the gods survive—
The white ideal fire
  That keeps my soul alive.

Now, at the wondrous hour,
  She leaves her star supreme,
And comes in the night's still power
  To touch me with a dream.

Sibyl of mystery
  On roads beyond our ken,
Softly she comes to me,
  And goes to God again.

EDWIN MARKHAM

GOD'S WORLD

O WORLD, I cannot hold thee close
    enough!
  Thy winds, thy wide gray skies!
  Thy mists that roll and rise!
Thy woods this autumn day, that ache and sag
And all but cry with color! That gaunt crag
To crush! To lift the lean of that black bluff!
World, World, I cannot get thee close enough!

Long have I known a glory in it all
  But never knew I this.
  Here such a passion is
As stretcheth me apart. Lord, I do fear

GOD'S WORLD

Thou'st made the world too beautiful this year.
My soul is all but out of me—let fall
No burning leaf; prithee, let no bird call.

EDNA ST. VINCENT MILLAY

From RENASCENCE

I KNOW not how such things can be,
I only know there came to me
A fragrance such as never clings
To aught save happy living things;
A sound as of some joyous elf
Singing sweet songs to please himself,
And, through and over everything,
A sense of glad awakening.
The grass, a-tiptoe at my ear,
Whispering to me I could hear;
I felt the rain's cool finger-tips
Brushed tenderly across my lips,
Laid gently on my sealèd sight,
And all at once the heavy night

RENASCENCE

Fell from my eyes and I could see,—

A drenched and dripping apple tree,

A last long line of silver rain,

A sky grown clear and blue again.

And as I looked a quickening gust

Of wind blew up to me and thrust

Into my face a miracle

Of orchard-breath, and with the smell,—

I know not how such things can be!—

I breathed my soul back into me.

Ah! Up then from the ground sprang I

And hailed the earth with such a cry

As is not heard save from a man

Who has been dead, and lives again.

About the trees my arms I wound;

Like one gone mad I hugged the ground;

I raised my quivering arms on high;

I laughed and laughed into the sky,

Till at my throat a strangling sob

Caught fiercely, and a great heart-throb

Sent instant tears into my eyes;

O God, I cried, no dark disguise

Can e'er hereafter hide from me

Thy radiant identity!

Thou canst not move across the grass

But my quick eyes will see Thee pass,

Nor speak, however silently,

But my hushed voice will answer Thee.

I know the path that tells Thy way

Through the cool eve of every day;

God, I can push the grass apart

And lay my finger on Thy heart!

The world stands out on either side

No wider than the heart is wide;

RENASCENCE

Above the world is stretched the sky,—
No higher than the soul is high.
The heart can push the sea and land
Farther away on either hand;
The soul can split the sky in two,
And let the face of God shine through.
But East and West will pinch the heart
That cannot keep them pushed apart;
And he whose soul is flat—the sky
Will cave in on him by and by.

EDNA ST. VINCENT MILLAY

A SONG OF TENDER THINGS

THE little lapping, loving things,
    How tenderly they lie,
Their bodies sacred to the sun
And mothered by the sky;
The gentle, purring, pretty things
With delicate, dear breast—
The kitten on the window ledge,
The squirrel in his nest—
The little, glossy, trembling things
With whimpering, soft cries,
I see God look at me sometimes
Out of their limpid eyes.
And often in the twilight hush

A SONG OF TENDER THINGS

I think I hear Him speak
Through fragile, frightened, furry things
That are so greatly weak.

The tiny, tender birdling things,
How wondrously they fly,
The flutter of God's happiness,
The laughter in His eye.
And all the bubbles of bright song
Flung from a thousand throats—
The bobolink's, the meadow lark's,
The thrush's liquid notes,
Oh, fields of buttercups are there—
Or so the story's told—
To catch the shower of sweet song
In chalices of gold.
The little, darting, chirping things

AMERICAN MYSTICAL VERSE

With downy wings and sweet,
I think they chatter oft of us
Who trudge with mortal feet,
And wonder why we seldom sing
And still more seldom play—
The rhythms of eternity
Flow through them all the day.

O Life that leaps within them all,
Mysterious and fine,
Thou hast a myriad shapes of light
Within this world of thine;
The stars, the flowers, the roads, the hills,
People and rocks and trees.
Thou hast a host of children, Life,
But none so dear as these.

ANGELA MORGAN

I HAVE MEAT

LIFE, who art bitter to my need
   And cruel to my body's cry;
Who mockest when thou dost not feed
And smilest when thy martyrs die,
Thou hast no terror nor defeat,
Thou hast no challenge to destroy
What burns within me, strong and sweet—
My heart's unalterable joy.

What should I ask of meat or wine
Who have the milk that madness spills?
From brimming breasts of April hills
My soul may draw a drink divine.

What should I seek of wine or food
That brain and muscle may not tire?

AMERICAN MYSTICAL VERSE

I, who am drunken with thy good

And eager with thine inner fire?

I, who may drain the sacred brew

Of human lore from age to age—

The splendor that Mohammed knew,

Savonarola's mystic rage—

The triumphs of the great and wise

Through centuries of sacrifice;

I, who may lave me in the stream

Of Homer's heart and Phidias' dream,

What other chalice need I know?

And what have I to do with bread

Who have this golden cup instead—

The faith that fired Galileo?

My veins are rivulets that find

The ocean surges of the race;

I HAVE MEAT

My freshened pulses keeping pace
To all the passion of mankind.
How weak the dull, material cup
How faint the frenzied moment's gain
To these high beauties that I sup
Poured from the world's delicious pain.
O flaming lovers everywhere,
You know no rapture that I miss.
My nerves melodiously aware
Behold me nourished by your bliss!
O heroes, streaming up the sky
Shedding your clay upon the sod,
My soul is richer as you die
And I am closer still to God!
As one who all-enchanted sips
An endless potion, deep and red,
The world's great goblet at my lips,

AMERICAN MYSTICAL VERSE

What should I seek of wine or bread?
Let me but feel the mighty whir
Of God's great pulses, strong and sure
Stupendous in my being stir—
And all my powers shall endure.

Life, who art cruel to my cry
And givest but a crust to eat,
Thine ardent lover still am I—
For I have meat!

ANGELA MORGAN

MANIFESTATIONS

LORD, who walked upon the sea,
       Is it you who pass
Softly in the grass
When a little wind blows over,
Scarcely bending down the clover?

Is this robe of blooming yours
Spread across the field,
That its hem has healed
Suddenly my bitter heart
With a virtue passing art?

And the high far touch of hills
On my narrow sight

223

AMERICAN MYSTICAL VERSE

Shedding vistaed light—
Is it your hand healing me
As the blind of Galilee?

Hilda Morris

DUSK

IT is impossible to be alone here, even in this
    little cabin room,

After beholding the Glory of God through the
    somber splendor of twilight loom,

And the violet dusk of the mountains quiver, and
    the Holy of Holies glow through the gloom.

Dusk as a brooding spirit whispered over the
    face of the harrowed field;

Dusk as a dim-winged dragon darkened over the
    bay where the flame-points reeled;

As an angel, veiled and flaming-sworded, watched
    at the gates of the unrevealed.

Over the bay the lights of the city, a thousand
    blossoms of yellow flame,
Gleamed and twinkled out of the blue and ash-
    gray darkness; and there came
A slow wind thence: a murmurous rumor: human
    passion, sadness, shame.

And I beheld God in the mountains; God in the
    iris glow of the sky;
And I beheld in the throbbing lights of the city,
    God in His agony—
A heart-beat; a lamentation; an impassioned, low,
    insatiate cry.

KENNETH MORRIS

SYMBOL

MY faith is all a doubtful thing,
  Wove on a doubtful loom,—
Until there comes, each showery spring,
  A cherry tree in bloom;
And Christ who died upon a tree
  That death had stricken bare,
Comes beautifully back to me,
  In blossoms, everywhere.

DAVID MORTON

NOT OVERLOOKED

THOUGH I am little as all little things,
  Though the stars that pass over my
    tininess are as the sands of the sea,
Though the garment of the night was made for
  a sky-giant and does not fit me,
Though even in a city of men I am as nothing,
Yet at times the gift of life is almost more than
  I can bear . . .
I laugh with joyousness: the morning is a blithe
  holiday:
And in the overrunning of my hardy bliss, praise
  rises for the very breath I breathe.

228

NOT OVERLOOKED

How soaked the universe is with life:

Not a cranny but is drenched:

Ah, not even I was overlooked!

JAMES OPPENHEIM

LISTEN

G O a little aside from the noise of the world:
     Go near to yourself . . .

Listen . . .

Ah, music, pulse-beats of Life, whispers of Death!

They were there all the time like a brook that is

    under the ground.

JAMES OPPENHEIM

I COULD WRITE THE PSALMS AGAIN

I COULD write the psalms again,
  I could raise on high a voice of thanks-
    giving,
I could pace the eastern hills and bid the gates
  lift,
Bid the gates lift that usher the dawn of the
  spirit . . .
For my joy is the joy unbidden, welling from
  the heart,
The joy of the Life that springs of itself from
  the inmost recesses
When in still loneliness self meets with self.

JAMES OPPENHEIM

HE WHOM A DREAM HATH POSSESSED

HE whom a dream hath possessed knoweth
no more of doubting,

For mist and the blowing of winds and the
mouthing of words he scorns;

Not the sinuous speech of schools he hears, but
a knightly shouting,

And never comes darkness down, yet he greeteth
a million morns.

He whom a dream hath possessed knoweth no
more of roaming;

All roads and the flowing of waves and the
speediest flight he knows,

HE WHOM A DREAM HATH POSSESSED

But wherever his feet are set, his soul is forever
   homing,
And going, he comes, and coming he heareth a
   call and goes.

He whom a dream hath possessed knoweth no
   more of sorrow,
At death and the dropping of leaves and the
   fading of suns he smiles,
For a dream remembers no past and scorns the
   desire of a morrow,
And a dream in a sea of doom sets surely the
   ultimate isles.

He whom a dream hath possessed treads the
   impalpable marches;
From the dust of the day's long road he leaps
   to a laughing star,

And the ruin of worlds that fall he views from
eternal arches,

And rides God's battlefield in a flashing and
golden car.

SHAEMAS O'SHEEL

THEY WENT FORTH TO BATTLE,
BUT THEY ALWAYS FELL

THEY went forth to battle, but they always
fell.

Their eyes were fixed above the sullen shields.

Nobly they fought and bravely, but not well,

And sank heart-wounded by a subtle spell.

They knew not fear that to the foeman yields,

They were not weak, as one who vainly wields

A futile weapon; yet the sad scrolls tell

How on the hard-fought field they always fell.

It was a secret music that they heard,

A sad sweet plea for pity and for peace,

And that which pierced the heart was but a word,

Though the white breast was red-lipped where
the sword
Pressed a fierce cruel kiss to put surcease
On its hot thirst, but drank a hot increase.
Ah they by some strange troubling doubt were
stirred,
And died for hearing what no foeman heard.

They went forth to battle but they always fell.
Their might was not the might of lifted spears.
Over the battle-clamor came a spell
Of troubling music, and they fought not well.
Their wreaths are willows and their tribute,
tears.
Their names are old sad stories in men's ears.
Yet they will scatter the red hordes of Hell,
Who went to battle forth and always fell.

Shaemas O'Sheel

A FRAGMENT

THIS wind upon my mouth, these stars I
    see;

The breathing of the night above the trees,

Not these nor anything my senses touch

Are real to me or worth the boon of breath.

But all the never-heard, the never-seen,

The just beyond my hands can never reach,

These have a substance that is stout and sure,

These brace the unsubstantial sliding world,

And lend the evanescent actual

An air of life, a tint of worth and meaning.

Shall dust, fortuitously blown into

A curve of moon or leaf or throat or petal

And seeding back to vacancy and dust,

Content my soul with its illiterate

And lapsing loveliness? Or tired knowledge

Make credible the hard decree of living?

O, I have heard a golden trumpet blowing

Under the night. Another warmth than blood

Has coursed, though briefly, through my
　　intricate veins.

Some sky is in my breast where swings a hawk

Intemperate for immortalities

And unpersuaded by the show of death.

I am content with that I can not prove.

WILLIAM ALEXANDER PERCY

OVERTONES

I HEARD a bird at break of day
Sing from the autumn trees;
A song so mystical and calm,
So full of certainties,
No man, I think, could listen long
Except upon his knees.
Yet this was but a simple bird
Alone, among dead trees.

WILLIAM ALEXANDER PERCY

TEARS

WHEN I consider Life and its few years—
    A wisp of fog betwixt us and the sun;
A call to battle, and the battle done
Ere the last echo dies within our ears;
A rose choked in the grass; an hour of fears;
The gusts that past a darkening shore do beat;
The burst of music down an unlistening street—
I wonder at the idleness of tears.
Ye old, old dead, and ye of yesternight,
Chieftains, and bards, and keepers of the sheep,
By every cup of sorrow that you had,
Loose me from tears, and make me see aright
How each hath back what once he stayed to weep;
Homer his sight, David his little lad!

LIZETTE WOODWORTH REESE

LORD, OFT I COME

LORD, oft I come unto Thy door,
But when Thou openest it to me,
Back to the dark I shrink once more,
Away from light and Thee.

Lord, oft some gift of Thee I pray;
Thou givest bread of finest wheat;
Empty I turn upon my way,
Counting a stone more sweet.

Thou bidst me speed; then sit I still;
Thou bidst me stay; then do I go;
Lord, make me Thine in deed and will,
And ever keep me so!

LIZETTE WOODWORTH REESE

241

THE WHITE COMRADE

UNDER our curtain of fire,
Over the clotted clods,
We charged, to be withered, to reel
And despairingly wheel
When the bugles bade us retire
From the terrible odds.

As we ebbed with the battle-tide,
Fingers of red-hot steel
Suddenly closed on my side.
I fell, and began to pray.
I crawled on my hands and lay
Where a shallow crater yawned wide;
Then I swooned. . . .

THE WHITE COMRADE

When I woke, it was yet day.

Fierce was the pain of my wound,

But I saw it was death to stir,

For fifty paces away

Their trenches were.

In torture I prayed for the dark

And the stealthy step of my friend

Who, stanch to the very end,

Would creep to the danger zone

And offer his life as a mark

To save my own.

Night fell. I heard his tread,

Not stealthy, but firm and serene,

As if my comrade's head

Were lifted far from that scene

Of passion and pain and dread;

As if my comrade's heart

In carnage took no part;

As if my comrade's feet

Were set on some radiant street

Such as no darkness might haunt;

As if my comrade's eyes,

No deluge of flame could surprise,

No death and destruction daunt,

No read-beaked bird dismay,

Nor sight of decay.

Then in the bursting shell's dim light

I saw he was clad in white.

For a moment I thought that I saw the
      smock

Of a shepherd in search of his flock.

Alert were the enemy, too,

THE WHITE COMRADE

And their bullets flew

Straight at a mark no bullet could fail;

For the seeker was tall and his robe was

      bright;

But he did not flee nor quail.

Instead, with unhurrying stride

He came,

And gathering my tall frame,

Like a child, in his arms . . . .

I slept,

And awoke

From a blissful dream

In a cave by a stream.

My silent comrade had bound my side.

No pain now was mine, but a wish that I

      spoke,—

A mastering wish to serve this man

Who had ventured through hell my doom

    to revoke,

As only the truest of comrades can.

I begged him to tell me how best I might

    aid him,

And urgently prayed him

Never to leave me, whatever betide;

When I saw he was hurt—

Shot through the hands that were clasped

    in prayer!

Then, as the dark drops gathered there

And fell in the dirt,

The wounds of my friend

Seemed to me such as no man might bear.

Those bullet-holes in the patient hands

Seemed to transcend

246

THE WHITE COMRADE

All horrors that ever these war-drenched
     lands
Had known or would know till the mad
     world's end.
Then suddenly I was aware
That his feet had been wounded, too;
And, dimming the white of his side,
A dull stain grew.
"You are hurt, White Comrade!" I cried.
His words I already foreknew:
"These are old wounds," said he,
"But of late they have troubled me."

ROBERT HAVEN SCHAUFFLER

PROVIDENCE

WHEN I was far from the sea's voice
   and vastness,

I looked for God in the days and hours and
   seasons.

But now, by its large and eternal tides surrounded,

I know I shall only find Him in the greater swing
   of the years.

For like the sea's are His mysteries, not to be
   learned from a single surf-beat.

No wave suffices Him for a revelation.

How like the sea's, that dower all lands with green
   and the breath of blossoms,

With dews that never have heard its deathless
   surges.

PROVIDENCE

Let me be patient, then—sure that stars are not
    jetsam tossing
On meaningless waters of waste Omnipotence.
Let me be patient, even when man is sunk in the
    storm of His purpose,
And swirled, a strangled corpse, under His ages.

CALE YOUNG RICE

SONNET

O WORLD, thou choosest not the better part!
It is not wisdom to be only wise,
And on the inward vision close the eyes,
But it is wisdom to believe the heart.
Columbus found a world, and had no chart,
Save one that faith deciphered in the skies;
To trust the soul's invincible surmise
Was all his science and his only art.
Our knowledge is a torch of smoky pine
That lights the pathway but one step ahead
Across a void of mystery and dread.
Bid, then, the tender light of faith to shine
By which alone the mortal heart is led
Unto the thinking of the thought divine.

GEORGE SANTAYANA

"COME, COURAGE, COME"

COME, Courage, come, and take me by the
    hand!
  I have a long and weary way to go,
  And what may be the end I do not know—
I do not understand.

Come, Courage, come, and take me by the hand!
  Be thou my mentor! Be my guide and stay!
  The path is one I may not fare by day;
It leads through night's dim land.

Come, Courage, come, and take me by the hand!
  Gird me with faith, the radiant faith to see
  Beyond the darkness—immortality;
Thus may the gulf be spanned.

Come, Courage, come, and take me by the hand!
CLINTON SCOLLARD

251

SANCTUARY

LET us put by some hour of every day
    For holy things!—whether it be when
    dawn
Peers through the window pane, or when the noon
Flames, like a burnished topaz, in the vault,
Or when the thrush pours in the ear of eve
Its plaintive monody; some little hour
Wherein to hold rapt converse with the soul,
From sordidness and self a sanctuary,
Swept by the winnowing of unseen wings,
And touched by the White Light Ineffable!

CLINTON SCOLLARD

IN AUTUMN

MINE eyes fill, and I know not why at all.

Lies there a country not of time and space—
Some fair and irrecoverable place
I roamed ere birth and cannot now recall?—
    A land where petals fall
On paths that I shall nevermore retrace?

Something is lacking from the wistful bow'rs,
  And I have lost that which I never had.
  The sea cries, and the heavens and sea are sad,
And love goes desolate, yet is not ours.
    Brown Earth alone is glad,
Robing her breast with fallen leaves and flow'rs.

AMERICAN MYSTICAL VERSE

High memories stir; the spirit's feet are slow,
 In nameless fields where tears alone are fruit,
 And voices of the wind alone transmute
The music that I lost so long ago.
  I stand irresolute,
Lonely for some one I shall never know.

GEORGE STERLING

"OMNIA EXEUNT IN MYSTERIUM"

I

THE stranger in my gates—lo! that am I,
   And what my land of birth I do not
      know,
   Nor yet the hidden land to which I go.
One may be lord of many ere he die,
And tell of many sorrows in one sigh,
   But know himself he shall not, nor his woe,
   Nor to what sea the tears of wisdom flow;
Nor why one star is taken from the sky.

An urging is upon him evermore,
   And though he bide, his soul is wanderer,
      Scanning the shadows with a sense of haste—
Where fade the tracks of all who went before:

A dim and solitary traveler

   On ways that end in evening and the waste.

II

How dumb the vanished billions who have died!

   With backward gaze conjectural we wait,

   And ere the invading Shadow penetrate,

The echo from a mighty heart that cried

Is made a sole memorial to pride.

   From out the night's inscrutable estate,

   A few cold voices wander, desolate

With all that love has lost or grief has sighed.

Slaves, seamen, captains, councilors and kings,

   Gone utterly, save for those echoes far!

   As they before, I tread a forfeit land,

Till the supreme and ancient silence flings

   Its pall between the dreamer and the star.

   O desert wide! O little grain of sand!

GEORGE STERLING

RETRIBUTION

WOOD of the Cross, you might have been
 Pale-budded then for spring;
Wood of the Cross, you might have shared
 New life with everything.

If there was need to cut you down,
 They might have made of you
A little house in a silent town
 Where dusky olives grew.

Lamb of the Cross, You might have been
 Alive for many a day,
Walking with those who held You dear
 Along some ancient way.

If there was need for You to die,
  Why did they kill You so?
Why did they make You tread the way
  That low men used to go?

Wood of the Cross, you might have died
  Ere many years had passed,
But now you will be blossoming
  As long as earth shall last.

Lamb of the Cross, You might have been
  A myth, a passing dream;
But now You are the Risen Lord
  Whom great and poor esteem.

VIOLET ALLEYN STOREY

THE TROUBADOUR OF GOD

I WALK the dusty ways of life
    But ever my heart beats high,
And my song ascends to the crystal tower
That pierces up through the sky.

For there is my love who holds my heart
Like a bird on silken chain,
Who smote my side with a gladsome wound
And slays me with sweetest pain,
Till the love of the fairest woman on earth
Is a paltry thing and vain.

I trudge at morn right merrily
For oh! my heart is young,

259

AMERICAN MYSTICAL VERSE

I give good words and a hand at need
To those I walk among,
But I long for the bliss of the bridal hour
When the vesper bell is rung.

Till then I sing as best I may
My love, so kind, so rare,
I mumble not in a monk's dark cell;
Nay, song is braver than prayer.
I go where my brothers may hear my voice
In the glow of the warm bright air.

And though I have never seen my Love
Yet the pulse of my faith is strong,
It fills all the world with loveliness
And it fills my heart with song.

Charles Wharton Stork

GOD, YOU HAVE BEEN TOO
GOD TO ME

GOD, you have been too good to me,
  You don't know what you've done.
A clod's too small to drink in all
The treasure of the sun.

The pitcher fills the lifted cup
And still the blessings pour ;
They overbrim the shallow rim
With cool refreshing store.

You are too prodigal with joy,
Too careless of its worth,
To let the stream with crystal gleam
Fall wasted on the earth.

Yet many thirsty lips draw near

And quaff the greater part!

There still will be too much for me

To hold in one glad heart.

CHARLES WHARTON STORK

PATMOS

ALL around him Patmos lies,
  Who hath spirit-gifted eyes,
Who his happy sight can suit
To the great and the minute.
Doubt not but he holds in view
A new earth and heaven new;
Doubt not but his ear doth catch
Strain nor voice nor reed can match:
Many a silver, sphery note
Shall within his hearing float.

All around him Patmos lies,
Who unto God's priestess flies:
Thou, O Nature, bid him see,
Through all guises worn by thee,

A divine apocalypse.

Manifold his fellowships:

Now the rocks their archives ope;

Voiceless creatures tell their hope

In a language symbol-wrought;

Groves to him sigh out their thought;

Musings of the flower and grass

Through his quiet spirit pass.

'Twixt new earth and heaven new

He hath traced and holds the clue,

Number his delights ye may not;

Fleets the year but these decay not.

Now the freshets of the rain,

Bounding on from hill to plain,

Show him earthly streams have rise

In the bosom of the skies.

Now he feels the morning thrill,

PATMOS

As upmounts, unseen and still,
Dew the wing of evening drops.
Now the frost, that meets and stops
Summer's feet in tender sward,
Greets him, breathing heavenward.
Hieroglyphics writes the snow,
Through the silence falling slow;
Types of star and petaled bloom
A white missal-page illume.
By these floating symbols fine,
Heaven-truth shall be divine.

All around him Patmos lies,
Who hath spirit-gifted eyes;
He need not afar remove,
He need not the times reprove,
Who would hold perpetual lease
Of an isle in seas of peace.

EDITH MATILDA THOMAS

265

HEADLAND ORCHARDS

I Will Send the Comforter

APRIL lit the apple-flower and waved it,
  Music nested on the spray,
Loudly called the lookout bird through rainbows,
  Earth was curving into May.

In that hour the light from hillside orchards
  Pierced him, and the heavens about
Opened, and before intense burning,
  Fire by fire his heart went out.

Flashing seas beyond the melted skymark
  Sang beneath another dome;
There his vision sailed to breathless knowledge,
  Sailed and found and drew back home.

266

HEADLAND ORCHARDS

Peace was in him from the starry motion,
    Then his breast received the sign;
At life's marriage feast the hidden lover,
    Master of the water and the wine.

Through his flesh the suns of power and beauty
    Warmed the moaning worlds to song;
Bread and healing from his broken body
    Fed the sky-bewildered throng.

So his spirit would have freed earth's music
    Radiant, captive, yearning, mute;
Swift he plucked and held up apple branches,
    Signals of the ripened fruit.

But the morning fell as leaves around him,
    And the clay unpurified
Mocked him, scourged him, till the dove-like glory
    Vanished from his wounded side.

AMERICAN MYSTICAL VERSE

Broken apple branches reaching sunward,
  Distant sea and no sail spread,
These remained, and clouds above the hillside,
  And the multitude unfed.

Yet his heart had found on one far island
  Where the high dream dipped its prow,
Arrowy odors of immortal apples,
  Raining from a golden bough.

Flame that led me in that hour of marvel,
  Shall we ever win again
Past the sea-line to the fruit and bring it
  Glorious for the hearts of men?

Helmsman, lover, I am empty-handed,
  Silent, empty, year on year,
But through all the skies my longing rises,
  Longing, longing. Will you hear?

HEADLAND ORCHARDS

THE COMFORTER SPEAKS

My beloved, I have never left you.

    Through your breath I breathe the night,

Through your veins my pulses flow in darkness,

    But in deeper worlds is light.

Deep within you sweep the burning splendors

    Brighter than your gaze can bear;

There I watch among the dawns within you,

    Sky on sky is folded there.

There I see the outward heavens open

    As the inner heavens unfold;

There, in tidal light, eternal islands

    Orb the ever-living gold.

On those inward shores are fountains lifting

    Powers and suns of endless might;

Songs of birth and gleams of dancers dancing

    Wash the ripening worlds with light.

AMERICAN MYSTICAL VERSE

Inward branches bear those fires of marvel
  Slowly in the lonely clay.
Whoso suffers with my flame shall slowly
  Find me in the inner day.

Wanderers deepening to those bright horizons
  Hidden by the bosom's wall,
Slowly as through music long forgotten
  Reach me and remember all.

Lonely one in silences unyielding,
  I am there whom tears conceal;
After victories I am in the stillness,
  Underneath despairs I heal.

Whoso suffers for my vision to bring it starlike
  Earthward out of dream at last,
Bears the fruit and deepens homeward from the
    darkness,
  Holy sailor of the starry vast.

RIDGELY TORRENCE

EYE-WITNESS

DOWN by the railroad in a green valley
     By dancing water, there he stayed awhile
Singing, and three men with him, listeners,
All tramps, all homeless reapers of the wind,
Motionless now and while the song went on
Transfigured into mages thronged with visions;
There with the late light of the sunset on them
And on clear water spinning from a spring
Through little cones of sand dancing and fading,
Close beside pine woods where a hermit thrush
Cast, when love dazzled him, shadows of music
That lengthened, fluting, through the singer's
     pauses

AMERICAN MYSTICAL VERSE

While the sure earth rolled eastward bringing
    stars
Over the singer and the men that listened
There by the roadside, understanding all.

A train went by but nothing seemed to be changed.
Some eye at a car window must have flashed
From the plush world inside the glassy Pullman,
Carelessly bearing off the scene forever,
With idle wonder what the men were doing,
Seeing they were so strangely fixed and seeing
Torn papers from their smeary, dreary meal
Spread on the ground with old tomato cans
Muddy with dregs of lukewarm chicory,
Neglected while they listened to the song.
And while he sang the singer's face was lifted,
And the sky shook down a soft light upon him

EYE-WITNESS

Out of its branches where like fruits there were

Many beautiful stars and planets moving,

With lands upon them, rising from their seas,

Glorious lands with glittering sands upon them,

With soils of gold and magic mold for seeding,

The shining loam of lands afoam with gardens

On mightier stars with giant rains and suns

There in the heavens; but on none of all

Was there ground better than he stood upon:

There was no world there in the sky above him

Deeper in promise than the earth beneath him

Whose dust had flowered up in him, the singer,

And three men understanding every word.

THE TRAMP SINGS:

I will sing, I will go, and never ask me why.

I was born a rover and a passer-by.

I seem to myself like water and sky,
A river and a rover and a passer-by.

But in the winter three years back
We lit us a night fire by the track,

And the snow came up and the fire it flew
And we couldn't find the warming room for two.

One had to suffer, so I left him the fire
And I went to the weather from my heart's
    desire.

It was night on the line, it was no more fire,
But the zero whistle through the icy wire.

As I went suffering through the snow
Something like a shadow came moving slow.

I went up to it and I said a word;
Something flew above it like a kind of bird.

EYE-WITNESS

I leaned in closer and I saw a face;
A light went round me but I kept my place.

My heart went open like an apple sliced;
I saw my Savior and I saw my Christ.

Well, you may not read it in a book,
But it takes a gentle Savior to give a gentle look.

I looked in his eyes and I read the news;
His heart was having the railroad blues.

Oh, the railroad blues will cost you dear,
Keeps you moving on for something that you
     don't see here.

We stood and whispered in a kind of moon;
The line was looking like May and June.

I found he was a roamer and a journey man
Looking for a lodging since the night began.

He went to the doors but he didn't have the pay,
He went to the windows; then he went away.

Says, "We'll walk together and we'll both be fed."
Says, "I will give you the 'other' bread."

Oh, the bread he gave and without money!
O drink, O fire, O burning honey!

It went all through me like a shining storm:
I saw inside me, it was light and warm.

I saw deep under and I saw above,
I saw the stars weighed down with love.

They sang that love to burning birth,
They poured that music to the earth.

I heard the stars sing low like mothers.
He said: "Now look, and help feed others."

I looked around, and as close as touch
Was everybody that suffered much.

EYE-WITNESS

They reached out, there was darkness only;
They could not see us, they were lonely.

I saw the hearts that deaths took hold of,
With the wounds bare that were not told of;

Hearts with things in them making gashes;
Hearts that were choked with their dreams'
    ashes;

Women in front of the rolled-back air,
Looking at their breasts and nothing there;

Good men wasting and trapped in hells;
Hurt lads shivering with the fare-thee-wells.

I saw them as if something bound them;
I stood there but my heart went round them.

I begged him not to let me see them wasted.
Says, "Tell them then what you have tasted."

AMERICAN MYSTICAL VERSE

Told him I was weak as a rained-on bee;
Told him I was lost.   Says: "Lean on me."

Something happened then I could not tell,
But I knew I had the water for every hell.

Any other thing it was no use bringing;
They needed what the stars were singing,

What the whole sky sang like waves of light,
The tune that it danced to, day and night.

Oh, I listened to the sky for the tune to come;
The song seemed easy, but I stood there dumb.

The stars could feel me reaching through them
They let down light and drew me to them.

I stood in the sky in a light like day,
Bringing in the word that all things say

EYE-WITNESS

Where the worlds hang growing in clustered
　　shapes
Dripping the music like wine from grapes.

With "Love, Love, Love," above the pain.
The vine-like song with its wine-like rain.

Through heaven under heaven the song takes root
Of the turning, burning, deathless fruit.

I came to the earth and the pain so near me,
I tried that song but they couldn't hear me.

I went down into the ground to grow,
A seed for a song that would make men know.

Into the ground from my roamer's light
I went; he watched me sink to night.

Deep in the ground from my human grieving,
His pain plowed in me to believing.

Oh, he took earth's pain to be his bride,
While the heart of life sang in his side.

For I felt that pain, I took its kiss,
My heart broke into dust with his.

Then sudden through the earth I found life
    springing;
The dust men trampled on was singing.

Deep in my dust I felt its tones;
The roots of beauty went round my bones.

I stirred, I rose like a flame, like a river,
I stood on the line, I could sing forever.

Love had pierced into my human sheathing,
Song came out of me simple as breathing.

A freight came by, the line grew colder,
He laid his hand upon my shoulder.

EYE-WITNESS

Says, "Don't stay on the line such nights,"

And led me by the hand to the station lights.

I asked him in front of the station-house wall

If he had lodging. Says, "None at all."

I pointed to my heart and looked in his face—

"Here—if you haven't got a better place."

He looked and he said: "Oh, we still must roam

But if you'll keep it open, well, I'll call it 'home.' "

The thrush now slept whose pillow was his wing.

So the song ended and the four remained

Still in the faint starshine that silvered them,

While the low sound went on of broken water

Out of the spring and through the darkness
    flowing

Over a stone that held it from the sea.

Whether the men spoke after could not be told,

A mist from the ground so veiled them, but they
  waited
A little longer till the moon came up;
Then on the gilded track leading to the mountains,
Against the moon they faded in common gold
And earth bore East with all toward the new
  morning.

RIDGELY TORRENCE

THREE PRAYERS FOR SLEEP AND WAKING

I. BEDTIME

ERE thou sleepest gently lay
Every troubled thought away:
Put off worry and distress
As thou puttest off thy dress:
Drop thy burden and thy care
In the quiet arms of prayer.

Lord, Thou knowest how I live,
All I've done amiss forgive:
All of good I've tried to do,
Strengthen, bless and carry through:
All I love in safety keep,
While in Thee I fall asleep.

II. Night Watch

If slumber should forsake
 Thy pillow in the dark,
 Fret not thyself to mark
How long thou liest awake.
There is a better way;
 Let go the strife and strain,
 Thine eyes will close again,
If thou wilt only pray.

Lord, Thy peaceful gift restore,
Give my body sleep once more:
While I wait my soul will rest
Like a child upon Thy breast.

III. New Day

Ere thou risest from thy bed,
Speak to God Whose wings were spread

THREE PRAYERS

O'er thee in the helpless night:
Lo, He wakes thee now with light!
Lift thy burden and thy care
In the mighty arms of prayer.

Lord, the newness of this day
Calls me to an untried way:
Let me gladly take the road,
Give me strength to bear my load,
Thou my guide and helper be—
I will travel through with Thee.

HENRY VAN DYKE

285

THE WAY

WHO seeks for heaven alone to save his
soul,

May keep the path, but will not reach the goal;

While he who walks in love may wander far,

But God will bring him where the Blessed are.

HENRY VAN DYKE

THE GREAT RIVER

"In la sua volontade è nostra pace"

O MIGHTY river! strong, eternal Will,
  Wherein the streams of human good
    and ill
Are onward swept, conflicting, to the sea!
The world is safe because it floats in Thee.

HENRY VAN DYKE

ONCE MORE

LADEN I come to that great Market-Place,
　　Where still unseen the secret Merchant
　　waits
To take our wares, our hoarded joys and tears
And life and death.　Not yet, not yet abates

That greed of his to sweep the harvest in.
Never a hearth or home or child or mate
But he must have it.　Let one grain of sand
For hidden building be, one dream elate

With separateness from Him, and He will fold
That thrilling voice of his within the winds.
Sweeter than music, wild as lover's flute
Piercing the night, his cadence rises, binds

ONCE MORE

Our willing to his Will. Then, then like fields

Whose ripened grain bows down, like hurrying
    leaves

When autumn's magic woos them from the trees,

Once more we strip our wood, we yield our
    sheaves.

G. O. WARREN

ACCEPTANCE *

I CANNOT think nor reason,
    I only know he came
With hands and feet of healing
And wild heart all aflame.

With eyes that dimmed and softened
At all the things he saw,
And in his pillared singing
I read the marching law.

I only know he loves me,
Enfolds and understands—
And oh, his heart that holds me,
And oh, his certain hands!

WILLARD WATTLES

---

* By permission from *Lanterns in Gethsemane* by Willard Wattles, copyright by E. P. Dutton and Company.

HAUNTED EARTH

HEAVEN at last
　　Is bared, and the whole world one
　　　　radiant room—
Black are the shadows, in great pools of gloom
　　　　By copse and thicket cast.

　　The cattle browse
With sound of gentle breathing, and their breath
Is mild in glimmering meadows, or beneath
　　　　Drooped branches, where they drowse;

　　While 'mongst the chill
Shadows, and cold, clear moonlight all about,
A single bat goes dipping in and out
　　　　Softly; and all is still.

AMERICAN MYSTICAL VERSE

Silence around,—
Save for a cricket! Lapped in slumb'rous peace
Lie hill and meadowland, the shining seas
Lap on them without a sound.

It is earth's cry
Lifted in adoration: the old dream,
Beauty, is with her, and her hour supreme
That goes so swiftly by.

Too well she knows
The sweet Illusion, from no earthly shore
Visitant, the bright word that evermore
Troubles her dark repose.

Her heart lies bare·—
Drunken, drunken, she lifts a dreamy breast;
Hour by hour, in rapture and unrest
Flows the unending prayer.

HAUNTED EARTH

The path of night
Reaches, from rim to rim, a radiant road
Whereon the exalted Beauty walks abroad
In wonder and wild light.

Upon what eyes,
Lifted in homesickness, now falls again
The loveliness that haunts the world with pain—
Remembering Paradise!

JOHN HALL WHEELOCK

THE FLESH AND THE DREAM

THE baffled dreamer, the defeated Christ
  That for your love upon the cross-tree
   hung—
O take Him to your bosom, give Him rest
Close at the wanton wonder of your breast,
 O carnal World, forever well and young!

JOHN HALL WHEELOCK

EXILE FROM GOD

I DO not fear to lay my body down
    In death to share
The life of the dark earth and lose my own,
    If God is there.

I have so loved all sense of Him, sweet might
    Of color and of sound,—
His tangible loveliness and living light
    That robes me 'round.

If to His heart in the hushed grave and dim
    We sink more near,
It shall be well—living we rest in Him.
    Only I fear

Lest from my God in lonely death I lapse,

And the dumb clod

Lose Him; for God is life, and death

perhaps

Exile from God.

JOHN HALL WHEELOCK

THE OTHER PLACE

("My soul, there is a country . . .")

THERE is a far-off, closest place
　　Where I stand tall as I was meant to be:
There I look into your gleaming face
And see the light that you would have me see:
There is not Space as we know Space,
For close your hand locks, your breath lies. . . .
(*O how merciful and honorable your face,*
How pure your eyes!)

My youth and age are one in me
(*There is not Time as we know Time*)
O look and know and see!
There are no miles to go, no steps to climb,

We see and hear, all-swift, all-far,

For God is all this Other Place,

God and the briefest flower, the oldest star!

(The fern I passed and did not wait to gather

When I was five, I bend and gather now,

And O how beautiful the fruit and bud and bloom

On this long-perished bough!)

I feel the fern's furred stem,

Smell the lost peach-bough's sun-hot sharp

    perfume,

I can touch you, touch them,

And love the soul that you were meant to have

And see that shattering, nighted hour's clear

    blue. . . .

O sometimes we reach through

With human eye and hand

THE OTHER PLACE

To all of this, and know

That once more we are in our own real land. . . .

This is a show,

This little three-wayed prison where we go,

And wavering veils called Present and called Past

Dream-woven lock us fast . . .

Come! We shall break this painted game at last,

Here is our own real sky!

(O how wonderful God's grace,

How long-, long-known His face!)

MARGARET WIDDEMER

BARTER *

IF in that secret place
   Where thou hast hidden it, there yet is lying
Thy dearest bitterness, thy fondest sin,
Though thou hast cherished it with hurt and
   crying,
Lift now thy face,
Unlock the bolted door and let God in
And lay it in His holy hands to take. . . .

(How such an evil gift can please Him so
I do not know)
But, keeping it for wages, He shall make
Thy foul room sweet for thee with blowing wind

---

* By permission from *Cross Currents* by Margaret Widdemer, copyright, 1921, by Harcourt Brace and Company, Inc.

BARTER

(He is so serviceable and so kind)
And set sweet water for thy soul's distress,
Instead of what thou hadst, of bitterness,
And He shall bend and spread
Green balsam boughs to make a scented bed
Soft for thy lying
Where thine own thorns pricked in. . . .

Who would not pay away his dearest sin
To let such service in?

MARGARET WIDDEMER

SONNET

THAT which made me was bred of ache
and bleeding,
Of ageless agony that shrieked and tore:
And since all this has gone into the kneading
My substance can endure a little more.
What if men labor for deceitful prizes,
Or if no prizes crown the thorny strife?
We know, beyond the last remote surmises,
That life itself is the reward of life.
We know each day goes deathward robed in
splendor,
That night is deep and still and ever dear,
That men are warm in friendship, women tender,

SONNET

And that their love brings brimming harvest
    here,
A bright rebirth before the old soul perish,
An immortality to touch and cherish.

CLEMENT WOOD

"O ECSTASY"

O ECSTASY of the remembering heart
    That makes of all time but one
      stretchèd day,
And brings us forward on life's glorious way
An hour or two before we shall depart!
And thus the whole world melts to timeless art,
    And we in the eternal moment stay;
    That is accomplished for which men pray,
And blunted is the ever-fatal dart.

Among the flowering ruins of old time
    I played with beauty's fragments; Death and
      Hope
Upon the dizzy stone beheld me climb

"O ECSTASY"

And in the acanthus-mantled marble grope;

I only heard the dawn Memnonian chime

'Mid the wild grasses and wild heliotrope.

George E. Woodberry

IMMORTAL LOVE

IMMORTAL Love, too high for my possess-
   ing—
  Yet, lower than these, where shall I find repose?
  Long in my youth I sang the morning rose,
By earthly things the heavenly pattern guessing!
Long fared I on, beauty and love caressing,
  And finding in my heart a place for those
  Eternal fugitives; the golden close
Of evening folds me, still their sweetness blessing.

Oh, happy we, the first-born heirs of nature,
  For whom the Heavenly Sun delays his light!
He by the sweets of every mortal creature

IMMORTAL LOVE

Tempers eternal beauty to our sight;

And by the glow upon love's earthly feature

Maketh the path of our departure bright.

George E. Woodberry

LUCIFER SINGS IN SECRET *

I AM the broken arrow
    From Jehovah's quiver;
He will not let me sorrow
For ever and ever.

He will give me a new feather
That is white, not red;
He will bind me together
With the hairs of his head.

My shaft will be jointed
Like the young springing corn;
My tip will be pointed
With a painted thorn.

He will be willing

LUCIFER SINGS IN SECRET

That I lift my voice,

Among all the killing

To make my choice;

To harry the wagons

Of the wicked's retreat;

To murder dragons

Who have licked my feet.

I shall choose the target

His arrow deserves;

I shall trace and mark it

In scarlet curves.

Small and bloody

As a fallen sparrow

My own dead body

Shall receive his arrow.

ELINOR WYLIE

(1)

THE END